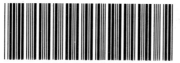

PERCEIVED IMPACT OF CHILDHOOD SEXUAL ABUSE ON ADULT RELATIONSHIP PARTNERS

Perceived Impact of Childhood Sexual Abuse on Adult Relationship Partners

Noelle S. Wiersma

Nova Science Publishers, Inc.

New York

For permission to use material from this book please contact us:
Telephone 631-231-7269; Fax 631-231-8175
Web Site: http://www.novapublishers.com

NOTICE TO THE READER

The Publisher has taken reasonable care in the preparation of this book, but makes no expressed or implied warranty of any kind and assumes no responsibility for any errors or omissions. No liability is assumed for incidental or consequential damages in connection with or arising out of information contained in this book. The Publisher shall not be liable for any special, consequential, or exemplary damages resulting, in whole or in part, from the readers' use of, or reliance upon, this material.

Independent verification should be sought for any data, advice or recommendations contained in this book. In addition, no responsibility is assumed by the publisher for any injury and/or damage to persons or property arising from any methods, products, instructions, ideas or otherwise contained in this publication.

This publication is designed to provide accurate and authoritative information with regard to the subject matter covered herein. It is sold with the clear understanding that the Publisher is not engaged in rendering legal or any other professional services. If legal or any other expert assistance is required, the services of a competent person should be sought. FROM A DECLARATION OF PARTICIPANTS JOINTLY ADOPTED BY A COMMITTEE OF THE AMERICAN BAR ASSOCIATION AND A COMMITTEE OF PUBLISHERS.

LIBRARY OF CONGRESS CATALOGING-IN-PUBLICATION DATA

Available Upon Request
ISBN: 978-1-60456-938-4

Published by Nova Science Publishers, Inc. ✦ New York

CONTENTS

PREFACE

Recently, increasing research and clinical attention has been directed toward the concerns of adult female survivors of childhood sexual abuse. Nonetheless, the relationship partners of these individuals have been largely overlooked in the trauma literature. It has been suggested that partners represent "secondary victims" who may experience significant distress as a result of their vicarious encounter with the trauma sustained by the primary survivor. These speculations, however, have been based almost exclusively on informal clinical observations, predominantly of males as adjunct participants in the therapy of female partners who have been raped in adulthood after their relationships with their partners were already established. Given these deficits, the present qualitative study investigated the perceived impact of the child sexual abuse experienced by female primary survivors on their current relationship partners. Six female survivors and their corresponding relationship partners participated in individual interviews of approximately 2 hours duration, during which they were asked to share their perceptions of the sequelae of the childhood sexual abuse on the partners as secondary survivors. Transcribed data were analyzed using the open and axial coding procedures of Strauss and Corbin's (1990) grounded theory method. Results consisted of emergent themes outlining the potential affective, cognitive, self-perceptual, somatic, sexual, academic/career, and social sequelae that may be encountered by the adult relationship partners of women who were sexually abused in childhood.

Chapter 1

INTRODUCTION

The issue of childhood sexual abuse has received substantive research and media attention over the past 25 years, predominantly describing its short- and long-term effects on female survivors and their process of recovery. Nonetheless, the adult relationship partners of those who have been sexually victimized in childhood continue to be largely overlooked in the trauma literature (Figley, 1983; Remer and Elliott, 1988a, 1988b). Only more recently has attention been given to the experiences of the men and women who form relationships with the primary survivors of childhood sexual abuse.

Of particular import is the suggestion that these relationship partners, as a by-product of their close association and empathic connection with a female primary survivor (Figley, 1988a; 1995), can become "secondary victims" or, ultimately, "secondary survivors" (Remer and Elliott, 1988a, p. 389) of her sexual trauma experienced during childhood. As a result of exposure to the primary survivor's disclosures of sexual trauma and/or reenactments of dynamics rooted in the traumatic events (McCann and Pearlman, 1990), it has been proposed that secondary victims may experience personal emotional arousal and distress, as well as problems in the relationship with the primary survivor, of varying degrees and kind (Brittain and Merriam, 1988).

However, much of the literature on secondary sexual trauma is limited to theoretical speculations based on informal clinical observations of secondary survivors as participants in support groups or as adjunct participants in the therapy of the primary survivor (Brittain and Merriam, 1988; Chauncey, 1994; Ferguson, 1991; Firth, 1997). In addition, most of this literature addresses the secondary sequelae of sexual trauma for partners of women raped in adulthood as opposed to partners of women sexually abused in childhood (Cohen, 1988; Emm and

McKenry, 1988; Remer and Elliott, 1988*a*, 1988*b*; Rodkin, Hunt, and Cowan, 1982; Silverman, 1978; 1992). There is a paucity of more systematic and empirical research in which partners as secondary survivors of childhood sexual abuse are the primary focus of study, and not just viewed as tangentially important because their reactions may impact the primary survivors (Figley, 1988b). Hence, as noted by Remer (1990) most of these works offer merely impressionistic data as a basis for their conclusions and recommendations.

In light of such deficits, Figley (1995) has decreed that the phenomenon of secondary victimization constitutes the "least studied and least understood aspect of traumatic stress" (p. 7). Remer and Ferguson (1995) have noted that inquiry into the essence of secondary responses to childhood sexual abuse truly constitutes a "nascent area" (p. 407) of research. Similarly, Beaton and Murphy (1995) have surmised that this field of inquiry may be viewed as pre-paradigmatic according to Kuhn's (1970) model of theory development. Nonetheless, it is crucial to learn about the "cost of caring" (Figley, 1995, p. 7) and the distress experienced by partners as a result of their significant relationships to primary survivors of childhood sexual abuse.

Progress in our understanding of partners as secondary survivors of sexual abuse is important for several reasons. First, it is widely recognized that social networks in general, and families in particular, can serve important preventative and restorative functions that promote mental health. Pilisuk and Parks (1986) have described such societal and familial contexts as a "healing web" (p. 1) with repercussions for the well being of traumatized persons. As noted by Harvey and colleagues (Harvey, Orbuch, Weber, Merbach, and Alt, 1992), "...too much importance cannot be placed on the critical role of a confidant in finding meaning, healing, and in creating hope" (p. 121). In this respect, then, the experiences and responses of secondary survivors may have important implications for the recovery of primary survivors (Silverman, 1978). The assumption is that those closest to the primary survivors, especially their partners who maintain day-to-day contact with them in a variety of contexts, may have a potentially facilitative or debilitating influence on their adjustment process. With respect to primary survivor adjustment, a problem may arise when partners are incapacitated or rendered less helpful by their own physical, emotional, or perceptual responses (Silverman, 1978).

Second, it is important to attend to and to examine the responses of partners of females sexually abused as children so that we may understand and remediate their own personal distress. Figley (1988b) has emphasized secondary victimization as a crucial topic in need of further research, noting that inquiry in the field of traumatic stress is properly concerned with all aspects of promoting recovery following highly stressful events such as victimization, regardless of the status of the person as a primary survivor, survivor family member or family system, or survivor-helping mental health professional. The experiences of these individuals are important and worthy of attention not only as they inform the healing process and treatment efforts with the primary survivors, but also in their own right (Figley, 1988b).

Third, investigation into the nature of secondary victimization in response to childhood sexual abuse is indicated because of its ultimate potential to inform the treatment process with such individuals and couples. Practitioners have begun to recognize the importance of working with the families of trauma survivors in order to assist the primary survivor, decrease distress in other family members, and prevent adverse family reactions to future stressful events (Burge and Figley, 1987; Figley, 1988a; Pilisuk and Parks, 1986). However, treatment efforts inclusive of secondary survivors have, of necessity, proceeded in the absence of much research or detailed information about the nature of their issues, concerns, and perspectives. Only by addressing this oversight will competent application of the most appropriate and efficacious therapeutic strategies with these populations be realized.

Finally, a number of authors have emphasized the "chiasmal effect" (Kishur and Figley, 1987, p. 1) of trauma as a kind of "contagion" (Chessick, 1978, p. 5) that transmits abuse-related affect, behavior, and cognition from the primary survivor to her supporters. The language of much of this work has tended to highlight similarities between the nature and degree of trauma experienced by the primary survivor and that experienced by the secondary survivor, as in the "shared trauma" (Silverman, 1978, p. 166) of rape for victimized women and their mates. Less often, the experiences and healing processes of adult female survivors of childhood sexual abuse and their relationship partners are described as "enmeshed," or "intertwined" (Remer, 1990, Chapter 3, p. 1). The latter would seem to imply that the repercussions of the abuse for the primary and secondary survivor may be more complementary, that is, they may be different but reciprocally related. Whether the impact of the abuse for secondary survivors is more like or unlike that experienced by the primary survivors, and under what circumstances, remains unclear.

These collective observations indicate that a more in-depth descriptive study of abuse sequelae for partners as secondary survivors is needed, one that is grounded in the data, is open to a broad range of possible responses to the abuse, and considers the perspectives of both secondary survivors and the adult female survivors of childhood sexual abuse who love them. This chapter presents a qualitative study investigating the sequelae of childhood sexual abuse for these secondary survivors. To provide important context, the long-term sequelae of childhood sexual abuse for primary survivors and the general phenomena of vicarious traumatization as well as secondary traumatic stress are briefly considered, and an extensive review of the limited research addressing abuse sequelae for the adult relationship partners of childhood sexual abuse survivors is presented.

Throughout, the term "sequelae" is used to acknowledge that popular terminology referring to the "effects" of childhood sexual abuse often implies a direct causal relationship between such experiences and subsequent mental health status that cannot be conclusively drawn on the basis of retrospective, non-experimental studies (Conte, 1985; Kilpatrick, 1987). The broad range of phenomena experienced by secondary and primary survivors as captured in this study can therefore be viewed more aptly as the sequelae, or things that occur subsequent to, the abuse.

Chapter 2

THE SEQUELAE OF CHILDHOOD SEXUAL ABUSE FOR ADULT FEMALES AS PRIMARY SURVIVORS

A comprehensive review of collective empirical findings confirms the common notion that the experience of sexual abuse in childhood may be associated with a wide range of problematic symptoms in adulthood for primary survivors. Among the most well documented adult sequelae of childhood sexual trauma are depression, self-destructive behavior, anxiety, feelings of isolation and stigma, poor self-esteem, and substance abuse (Beitchman et al., 1992; Browne and Finkelhor, 1986; Cahill et al., 1991; Green, 1993; Kilpatrick, 1987; Sheldrick, 1991). Although there is less consistency in findings regarding sexual functioning, it appears that a variety of sexual problems such as a lack of sexual enjoyment, sexual dysfunction, low sexual self-esteem, and partial or total avoidance of sexual activity may result for at least some adult female survivors.

Similarly, a meta-analytic review of the long-term sequelae of childhood sexual abuse for women implicated the symptoms of anxiety, anger, depression, revictimization, self-mutilation, sexual problems, substance abuse, suicidality, impairment of self-concept, interpersonal problems, obsessions and compulsions, dissociation, post-traumatic stress responses, and somatization as significant correlates of sexual abuse (Neumann, Houskamp, Pollock, and Briere, 1996). Given the nature of these difficulties, consequently poor interpersonal and marital relationships among child abuse survivors also may result (Browne and Finkelhor, 1986), and thus the study of their adult relationship partners as secondary survivors is indicated.

At the same time, existing reviews of the childhood sexual abuse literature indicate that there is a greater likelihood that poor psychological outcomes in adulthood will be associated with longer duration of abuse, multiple incidents of abuse, use of physical force or violence, perpetration by an adult, perpetration by a male, perpetration by one's father or stepfather, removal from the family home, or a lack of supportive responses by family members (Browne and Finkelhor, 1986; Russell, 1986). Evidence from these studies regarding age of onset, extent of disclosure, or abuse by non-relatives or relatives other than a father or stepfather is more equivocal. Unlike Browne and Finkelhor (1986), a survey of the literature by Beitchman and colleagues (1992) indicated a relationship between the specific nature of the sexually abusive acts and long-term impact as experienced by adult female survivors. Differentiating among studies based on types of outcome measures employed, these authors reported that genital or oral-genital intercourse is associated with a greater felt-sense of harm or trauma by adult female survivors, but not necessarily with more objective measures of their psychological functioning or adjustment.

Thus, a variety of intervening variables may be important in accounting for the adult mental health status of primary survivors, and the experience of childhood sexual abuse might best be viewed as a predisposing factor or potential contributor to some degree of impaired functioning in adulthood, with a range of moderating factors and possible outcomes. Although it is logical to assume that similar variables moderate abuse sequelae for secondary survivors, there is limited existing research to support that claim.

Chapter 3

VICARIOUS TRAUMATIZATION

The earliest attention afforded the concept of vicarious traumatization addressed the indirect influence of war-related combat on the veteran's family (Hill, 1949). Subsequently, this construct has been extended to a variety of traumatic events and trauma survivors. These include victims of sexual and nonsexual crimes, genocide (Lev-Wiesel and Amir, 2001), as well as natural disasters (Davis and Friedman, 1985; Drabek, Kay, Erickson, and Crowe, 1975). It also has been proposed that a variety of individuals may experience vicarious traumatization in the course of their employment, including workers in the fields of law enforcement (Kroes, 1976), medicine (Lipp, 1980; Rose and Rosow, 1973), emergency services (Hartsough, 1985; Mitchell, 1985; Summey, 2001), and mental health services (Chessick, 1978; Ghahramanlou and Brodbeck, 2000; Sexton, 1999). Almost all of this work is based on a posttraumatic stress model of vicarious trauma.

POSTTRAUMATIC STRESS RESPONSES TO VICARIOUS TRAUMA

The predominant model for understanding vicarious traumatization focuses on secondary reactions to extreme stressors among "victim associates" (Figley, 1986, p. 5). As noted by Figley (1986, 1988a), the vicarious trauma that can accrue to family members of persons who have experienced very stressful events has now been recognized by the *Diagnostic and Statistical Manual of Mental Disorders* (American Psychiatric Association, 1987; 1994). In particular, "serious threat or harm to one's children, spouse, or other close relatives and friends"

(American Psychiatric Association, 1987, p. 250) and "learning about unexpected or violent death, serious harm, or threat of death or injury experienced by a family member or other close associate" (DSM-IV, American Psychiatric Association, 1994, p. 424) are now included among the diagnostic criteria for Posttraumatic Stress Disorder (PTSD).

On this basis, Figley (1995) proposed a Secondary Traumatic Stress Disorder (STSD) to be applied in instances where the empathic induction of another's traumatic experiences results in "compassion fatigue" (p. 5) and considerable distress. Suggested diagnostic criteria for the experience of Secondary Traumatic Stress Disorder largely parallel those of PTSD and include (a) the experience of a stressor outside the range of usual human experiences, such as a serious threat to a traumatized person, (b) re-experiencing of the traumatized person's event in the form of recollections, dreams, or sudden re-experiencing or reminders, (c) avoidance or numbing of reminders, including efforts to avoid thoughts, feelings, activities, or situations, psychogenic amnesia, decreased interest in activities, detachment/estrangement, decreased affect, or sense of a foreshortened future, and (d) persistent arousal, marked by difficulty sleeping, irritable or angry outbursts, trouble concentrating, hypervigilance with respect to the traumatized person, exaggerated startle response, and physiological reactions to trauma-related cues (Figley,1995). As noted by Finkelhor (1987), however, PTSD represents only one of many possible responses to the trauma of childhood sexual abuse, and may not fully capture many other important aspects of such an experience for primary survivors. It is therefore reasonable to assume that STSD may be limited in its explanatory power for secondary survivors as well. The present investigation, therefore, considered other variants of response that may occur among secondary survivors in addition to those represented by the rather rigid diagnostic criteria of PTSD.

THE SEQUELAE OF CHILDHOOD SEXUAL ABUSE FOR PARTNERS OF ADULT FEMALE SURVIVORS: A REVIEW OF EXISTING LITERATURE

Compared to the research regarding partners of rape survivors, literature addressing the experiences of partners of childhood sexual abuse survivors is even less prevalent. Study of these individuals is almost entirely descriptive or conceptual in nature, and based primarily on the clinical work of the respective authors with heterosexual (Barnett, 1993; Blume, 1990; Hansen, 1991; Maltas and

Shay, 1995; Maltz, 1988; Maltz and Holman, 1990; Miller and Sutherland, 1999; Reid, Mathews, and Liss, 1995) or lesbian (Hall, 1999; Kerewsky and Miller, 1996; Smolover, 1996) couples. There are also a number of self-help books written for primary survivors of childhood sexual abuse with sections pertaining to their significant others (Bass and Davis, 1988) as well as some addressed directly to the secondary survivors (Davis, 1991; De Beixedon, 1995; Engle, 1991; Gil, 1993; Graber, 1991; Landry and Bear, 1991; Spear, 1991; Stark, 1993). Based predominantly on clinical observations about the general concerns of partners of childhood sexual abuse victims, these texts consist chiefly of education regarding the effects of sexual abuse for primary survivors, advice about how to assist the primary survivors, and an emphasis on the importance of secondary survivor self-care.

In one early study, Cohen (1988) conducted an open-ended support group for male partners of female survivors of either childhood sexual abuse or rape in adulthood. Approximately five men, ranging in age from 21 to 50, regularly attended weekly 2-hour meetings, with a total of 15 different participants attending at least once over the course of a 5-month period. Recurrent themes occurring in unstructured group discussion, derived from the progress notes and recollections of the author as the group facilitator, included frustration, concern, helplessness, anger, and resentment in the context of experiencing the survivor's anger, feeling unable to assist the primary survivor, and submerging personal needs in favor of the needs of the primary survivor.

Cohen (1988) also observed that many members of the group gained insight into their situations, became more empathic and open, learned new coping strategies, explored new ways of behaving and interacting with the primary survivor, and began to feel less depressed, anxious, and alone over the course of the group work. Both the men and some of their partners, who were being seen in a separate support group for female primary survivors, verbally reported improvements in their relationships, especially in the areas of communication, empathy, and anger control. As a result, Cohen (1988) concluded that it is plausible to infer that positive changes in partner-victim relationships have a positive impact on the victim's recovery, although the study did not empirically test this assertion and no control group, standardized pre- or post-measures, or recognized method of qualitative data analysis was utilized.

Similarly, Brittain and Merriam (1988) offered groups for partners of childhood sexual abuse survivors using three basic group formats. The first, a supportive-educational group with male-female co-leaders, was a "drop-in" model in which attendance was not required. Each meeting of six or fewer partners lasted 1 1/2 hours, and a total of 17 individuals attended over a 9-month period. These participants included one female partner of a male primary survivor, although no attempt was made within the study to differentiate the nature of her specific experience from that of other group members. This reflects the broader tendency notable in the vicarious trauma literature to treat all secondary survivors the same, irrespective of demographic variables or type of trauma. The standard format was a 10-week course of 1 1/2 hour meetings requiring a commitment to weekly attendance. A syllabus and educational materials were provided by the male facilitator, and one of the four regularly attending male partners completed the course. The third group format consisted of a half-day weekend workshop with an educational and supportive focus. Ten partners, including one female partner of a male survivor and one female partner in a lesbian relationship, participated. Once again, no further consideration was afforded the experience of the female participant who was in a relationship with a female primary survivor. In all, a total of 31 partners were included in these three group modalities.

In these contexts, a number of reactions were observed among partners as secondary survivors of childhood sexual abuse, including guilt, inadequacy, rage, loneliness, defensiveness, engaging in compulsive behaviors, uneasiness about divulging the primary survivor's abuse history, confusion about the primary survivor's current attitudes and behavior, problems dealing with relationship conflict, a sense of threat when the primary survivor discusses the abuse with persons other than himself, a negative view of the primary survivor's counseling or counselor, and an expectation that the primary survivor concede to secondary survivor needs. Self-report of these individuals during the course of the group work indicated that the primary benefit of participation was a decrease in social isolation and a sense of relief in learning that others shared their difficulties and feelings. A subset of these partners also reported learning new skills of emotional expression and empathy and a new understanding of issues related to childhood sexual abuse. On the basis of these observations, Brittain and Merriam (1988) proposed two major subgroups of partners of sexual abuse survivors, including (a) those who are otherwise psychologically well-adjusted, motivated to learn about childhood sexual abuse, and able to improve their relationships to the primary survivor, and (b) those who are unable to assist the primary survivor or improve their relationships because of their own problems or histories of family dysfunction. Once again, however, the reported trends are based on cursory, informally derived impressions of the authors rather than an in-depth formal analysis of data pertaining to participants.

Likewise, Luepker and O'Brien (1989) detailed a number of salient issues regarding secondary victimization emerging within the context of a support group for spouses of women who had experienced childhood incest or adult sexual abuse by previous therapists. This group was open-ended and ongoing, meeting three times per month, with an average size of four members. The number of meetings attended by individual participants ranged from six sessions to continuous involvement for approximately one year. No distinction was made by the authors between these two subgroups of secondary survivors (i.e., childhood incest or adult sexual victimization by therapist), either with respect to treatment procedures within the support group setting or with respect to the nature of their concerns.

To the contrary, Luepker and O'Brien (1989) emphasized the similarity of issues across group members, as determined by interviews with the group leader, and presented relevant group themes reportedly experienced by all participants. In particular, these categories of experience involved feelings of isolation (e.g., lack of information regarding sexual abuse and its effects on secondary survivors, lack of others outside the marriage with whom they could openly discuss their feelings), confusion and ambiguity (e.g., questioning the extent of the primary survivor's participation in and responsibility for the abuse), anger and rage (e.g., violent retribution fantasies against perpetrators or harassment, obscenities and threats directed toward the perpetrators, anger with the primary survivor), loss and grief (e.g., loss of sexual functioning or enjoyment, loss of dreams or vision for marriage, emotional or physical loss of the primary survivor who temporarily left or was perceived as preoccupied with her own struggles, loss of self-esteem), and feelings of helplessness, frustration, and impatience (e.g., with the legal system, with their own inability to assist the primary survivor).

Chauncey (1994) provided a similar outline of the major concerns expressed by 20 male partners of female childhood sexual abuse survivors in the context of a series of support group interventions conducted over a 3-year period. Each group met for 12 weeks and had four to six members. Group participants, who were mostly professionals and college graduates, ranged in age from 20 to 55 years, with current relationship durations of 1 to 30 years. A predominant concern of these individuals focused on conflicts about expressing needs, including balancing their own needs for attention, nurturance, integrity, and autonomy with their desire or obligation to help the primary survivors, fear or hesitancy with respect to verbalizing needs that might overwhelm or distress the primary survivors, or fear of being perceived as abusive for expressing needs that might conflict with those of the primary survivors.

A second issue emerging from the work of Chauncey (1994) centered on difficulties with closeness, as male partners perceived themselves to be shut out by the anxiety, flashbacks, anger, withdrawal, or excessive busyness of the primary survivors. In response, despite their empathy for the primary survivors' feelings and need for self-protective distance, male partners expressed feelings of hurt, frustration, puzzlement, sadness, helplessness, and longing related to their attempts to feel close to their mates. Chauncey (1994) suggested that the men might have experienced an unconscious fear of closeness that was projected onto the primary survivors, but that their conscious experience was one of pain and distress.

A third theme among secondary survivors involved difficulties with spontaneity or unpredictability (Chauncey, 1994). This theme was reported as relevant to both the secondary survivors' behavior (e.g., a sense of "walking on eggshells", p. 672, fear of frightening the primary survivors, feelings of tension and responsibility for keeping the primary survivors relaxed and "on an even keel", p. 672) and to the primary survivors' behavior. The latter was often viewed as inconsistent and unpredictable by the male partners, who described difficulties with not knowing what's going to "set her off" (Chauncey, 1994, p. 672) or trying to divine exactly what the primary survivor wants at the moment.

A fourth theme reported by Chauncey (1994) focused on struggles of male secondary survivors with anger (also described as irritation, frustration, and resentment) as well as conflicting feelings of guilt and shame regarding such angry emotions. Particular foci of anger included problems getting their own needs and feelings acknowledged or met, rage and a sense of powerlessness vis à vis the perpetrator, or displacement of anger felt toward the primary survivors. Secondary survivors reported alternate means of venting anger, including writing, exercising, and engaging in other hobbies to yield the satisfaction previously sought in their relationships. As noted by Chauncey (1994), most male partners in this sample voiced extreme reluctance to show their angry feelings to the primary survivors.

A fifth theme for secondary survivors as described by Chauncey (1994) related to questions about how to deal with other family members, including whether or not to confront the perpetrator, whether or not to disclose the abuse to other relatives or to refrain from talking about what happened, and how to parent their own children to ensure healthy psychological development. An additional theme among secondary survivors involved issues related to the primary survivors' recovery processes, such as questioning the length and extent of eventual recovery, feelings of hopelessness, and a desire for more definitive knowledge about sexual abuse recovery (Chauncey, 1994). A final theme for these male partners centered on sexual difficulties, including lack or infrequency of sexual intercourse, feelings of hurt and rejection, confusion regarding the primary survivors' responses during sex, and a sense of having "shut off" (Chauncey, 1994, p. 673) sexual desire.

A long-term group for 16 male partners of female childhood sexual abuse survivors who met monthly over a 4 ½ year period identified similar concerns for these individuals (Barcus, 1997). These included a sense of waiting out the wife's struggles, avoidance of the issues through work or other forms of distancing, isolation from others and a sense of social embarrassment, relationship conflict attributed to the wife's abuse-related anger, increased parenting responsibilities, anger or frustration at the effects of the abuse, confusion, and an increase in empathy toward the primary survivor.

With a slightly different emphasis, Reid, Wampler, and Taylor (1996) examined husbands' responses to the therapy sought by their wives who were survivors of childhood sexual abuse. Based on a qualitative analysis of interview data from 17 couples, emergent themes addressed aspects of therapy that were perceived to be negative and, less frequently, those that were perceived to be beneficial. Specifically, emergent themes regarding perceived detriments of the primary survivor's therapy for the secondary survivor included a sense of alienation from the therapy process and encouraged by the therapist, impatience with the healing process and the continual focus on the primary survivor, and feeling blamed for the abuse, resulting in confusion helplessness, hurt, and/or anger and emotional distance. For secondary survivors, perceived benefits of the primary survivor's therapy included relief and decreased confusion resulting from the explanation of the primary survivor's behaviors in light of the abuse. For the secondary-primary survivor relationship, difficulties in communication (including a sense of betrayal when the primary survivor withholds information related to the abuse), alienation, sexual intimacy, other physical contact, and extended family relationships were reported by the husbands.

Bacon and Lein (1996) also conducted focus groups with six partners of childhood sexual abuse survivors to examine their marital relationships with abuse survivors and the impact of the primary survivors' therapy on the secondary survivors. In these groups, the men described problems with their sexual relationships such as sexual rejection and infrequent sexual activity or nonsexual touch, confusion about the source of difficulties in the relationship that lessened upon disclosure, loss of the initial relationship with the primary survivor that preceded her disclosure, anger at abuse-related relationship problems, and being identified with the perpetrator due to physical and behavioral similarities perceived by the primary survivor. An unknown number of men also reported a change in their faith in relationships in general and a mistrust of apparent positive changes in the primary survivor that led to distancing. Themes related to her therapy included perceived benefits and hopefulness, financial hardship, feelings of exclusion and jealousy, and feeling unfairly judged by the therapist.

Some of the most relevant research for the purposes of the present study is that of Ferguson (1991; 1993) regarding the subjective experiences of men in intimate relationships with female survivors of childhood sexual abuse. In a preliminary ethnographic study, Ferguson (1991) conducted individual interviews with seven men who were partners of adult female survivors. Participants, including six European-Americans and one African-American, ranged in age from early 20s to mid-60s, and had been coupled with the survivor for periods varying from 1 to 30 years. Semi-structured interviews, lasting between one and two hours, were loosely guided to illuminate participants' thoughts, feelings and behaviors associated with their situation as a secondary survivors, concerns and perceptions regarding their relationships, and their perspectives regarding the possibility that the primary survivors' history of abuse had influenced their relationships. Interviews were transcribed and reread several times, until themes reportedly emerged from the data, although no further information regarding the method of qualitative data analysis or auditing procedures was reported.

Ferguson's (1991) interview data resulted in four basic categories of themes, including relationship problems, attributions regarding influences on the relationship, individual concerns and responses, and beliefs about sex and sexual abuse. With respect to the category of relationship problems, anger and specific social obstruction (i.e., the blocking or hindering of attainment of personal needs or enjoyment from relationships) emerged as universal themes across participants. Other themes within this category, listed in descending rank order of number of subjects reporting the experience (n), included sexual problems such as sexual dissatisfaction or sexual interference of the primary victims' flashbacks (n = 6), communication difficulties of a general nature and as specifically regards sex or sexual abuse (n = 6), parenting disagreements (n = 6), feelings of rejection among male partners (n = 4), lack of trust (n = 4), and divorce or separation, with four participants who were no longer in relationships with the primary survivors.

A second major category of Ferguson's (1991) themes pertained to the men's attributions regarding influences on their relationships with the primary survivors. One specific theme within this category pertained to the men's belief that sexual abuse had a significant impact on their current relationships, by contributing to sexual problems, a lack of intimacy, and neglect of secondary survivors' needs in favor of primary survivors' needs (n = 7). Other themes in this category included the perceived influence (either positive or negative) of therapy on the relationship (n = 7), other influences on the relationship such as the secondary survivors' preexisting dysfunction or coexisting problems of the primary survivors (n = 5), and the influence of sexual abuse on reasons for original interpersonal attraction, including perceptions that the primary survivors' chose them as protectors, father figures, or means of escape (n = 4).

A third category of themes emanating from Ferguson's (1991) study related to the men's own individual concerns and responses as secondary survivors. Lack of social support (n = 7) and problems conversing about the abuse with others (n = 6) were notable themes within this category. Another theme involved the nature of the men's responses to the primary survivors' initial disclosures of childhood sexual abuse, such as support, empathy, victim blaming, disbelief, or anger at the perpetrator (n = 7). A further prominent theme in this category included a heightened awareness concerning sex role beliefs and behaviors or a decrease in stereotypical or traditionally male beliefs (n = 6). A related theme addressed the impact of secondary survivor status on worldview, such as adopting a darker view of human nature, rejecting organized Christianity, deepening spiritual beliefs (n = 5), and a theme of altered attitudes toward children and child-rearing (n = 2). Perception of the impact of childhood sexual abuse on the primary survivors constituted an additional relevant theme in this grouping (n = 6), with reports of sexual disinterest, confusion, promiscuity, persistent fears of their lives being in jeopardy, fear of loud noises, multiple personality disorder, fear of physically abusing their own children, or fear of men among the primary survivors. A theme of offering advice to other men who are secondary survivors also was noted in this cluster (Ferguson, 1991), and consisted of recommendations to seek support and education, to be supportive and empathic for the primary survivors, to attend to one's own needs as a secondary survivor, or to refrain from relationships with primary survivors (n = 6). An additional theme concerned responses to the primary survivors' dissociation, such as stress, avoidance, anger, helpfulness, or helplessness (n = 6). The last related theme consisted of the men's perceptions of the impact of the primary survivors' history of childhood sexual abuse on self as secondary survivor, such as making him more perceptive, more in tune with sadness and anger, more isolated from other men, less self-confident due to sexual difficulties, or more protective of women and children (n = 3).

A final cluster of Ferguson's (1991) themes concerned the male partner's beliefs about sex and sexual abuse. The two themes within this category included attitudes toward sexual abuse in general (e.g., increased understanding of the issue, continued subscription to conventional myths), and attitudes toward sex specifically within the context of the relationship with the primary survivors (e.g., the importance of sex to intimacy, refraining from initiating sex due to rejections).

Although Ferguson's (1991) study provides some interesting insights regarding the experiences of these individuals, only the secondary survivor's perspective is considered, despite the fact that the primary survivor's perspective is likely essential to the relationship concerns purported to be of interest. In addition, this manuscript remains unpublished and it is unclear from the description provided whether formal methods of qualitative data analysis were employed and, if so, which ones, thus leaving the credibility of the study an open question.

In a subsequent study, Ferguson (1993) was one of the few researchers in this area of inquiry to use a quasi-experimental design and standardized assessment instruments. Specifically, Ferguson explored the extent to which the male partners of women sexually abused in childhood perceive that their own needs are met within their relationships. The study also addressed the nature of these individuals' worldviews and attributions regarding misfortune, and whether they experience greater relationship dissatisfaction and distress than their male counterparts who are not secondary survivors of childhood sexual abuse. A total of 123 male participants returned anonymous 30-minute survey questionnaires obtained in mental health clinic waiting rooms or via response to newspaper advertisements. Thirty-nine of these surveys were excluded from data analysis due to the participants' own histories of childhood sexual abuse, adult sexual assault of self or partners, inadequate relationship duration (less than six months), or insufficient age (less than 18 years).

Interestingly, there were also 147 questionnaires returned by women that were apparently not subjected to analysis, although it is unclear whether these women were primary survivors in relationships with the male participants or other women in relationships with primary survivors. Therefore, despite the importance of multiple perspectives regarding relationship issues, Ferguson's (1993) investigation misses a significant opportunity to provide information regarding the perspective of females who are primary or secondary survivors of childhood sexual abuse in relationships.

The remaining 84 participants were classified into three groups, including a group of 27 men in relationships with female survivors currently in therapy, a comparison group of 19 men in relationships with females currently in therapy but without a known history of childhood sexual abuse, and a control group of 38 men in relationships with females not currently in therapy and without a known history of childhood sexual abuse. These three groups were statistically compared, via analysis of variance, on adaptations of existing measures of relationship satisfaction, specific social obstruction, sexual satisfaction, relationship trust, belief in a just world, and personal distress. No statistically significant differences were observed between groups with the exception that male partners of childhood sexual abuse survivors rated their female partners' as more distressed than did male partners of non-abuse therapy participants or non-therapy participants.

However, Ferguson's (1993) study was subject to a number of methodological limitations, including relatively small sample size resulting in limited statistical power, similarity between the intended control group and the experimental group with respect to reasons female partners were reportedly seeking therapy (i.e., female partners of both groups seeking treatment for relationship problems and stress), use of adapted measurement instruments with unknown psychometric properties, and failure to consider stage of therapy or healing of the male participants or their female partners that may influence current reported distress. Thus, while laudable, this empirical effort may be somewhat premature in some respects. For example, the problem checklist used by male partners to record their own distress and the distress of partners consisted of a 24-item listing of general problems (i.e., depression, low self-esteem, nervousness/anxiety) rated on a 4-point scale from never (0) to often (3) experienced. To the extent that such a limited general sampling of diffuse problems fails to adequately capture the specific experience of male partners as secondary survivors of childhood sexual abuse, researchers will indeed be unlikely to assess relevant difficulties and to detect differences between these individuals and other comparison groups.

A similar problem with the use of standardized assessments to capture the experiences of male partners of childhood sexual abuse survivors was observed in the earliest empirical study with this population (Burgoff, 1993). In this unpublished doctoral dissertation, responses of these secondary survivors on measures of global distress and nine specific symptom dimensions that were not specific to sexual or vicarious sexual trauma showed no statistically significant elevation. In their responses to open-ended survey questions regarding abuse effects, however, secondary survivors reported extensive effects on their relationships including sexual problems (e.g., the need for careful negotiation around sexual expression, decreased spontaneity, guilt regarding one's own sexuality, decreased frequency of sexual contact, relationship conflict regarding sexual issues), decreased emotional intimacy, communication struggles, financial hardship, parenting issues, reduced social ties, and difficulties coping with the fears, mistrust, and anger of the primary survivor resulting in emotional fatigue. One quarter of these participants also noted some positive influence of working through the abuse in terms of potential for personal growth and deeper intimacy with the primary survivor. In addition, perceived social support was negatively correlated with global distress, depression, interpersonal sensitivity, and psychoticism.

Surprisingly, only two empirical studies to date address the systemic effects of trauma by examining survivors of childhood sexual abuse and their relationship partners within the confines of the same study. Specifically, Nelson and Wampler

(2000) compared 96 treatment-seeking couples with a history of childhood physical or sexual abuse in one or both partners with a control group of 65 treatment-seeking couples without any abuse history. On measures of relationship satisfaction and family cohesion, couples comprised of at least one partner with a history of sexual and/or physical abuse scored significantly lower than did couples without a history of such abuse, and significantly higher on individual stress symptomology. Of particular interest was the fact that there were no significant differences observed between male or female individuals with a history of physical or sexual abuse and their non-abused partners on measures of individual stress symptoms, relationship satisfaction, and family adjustment, thereby demonstrating indirect support for secondary trauma theory.

Similarly, Nelson and Wampler (2002) compared 15 couples in which the female partner was a survivor of childhood sexual abuse and a control group of 17 couples with no abuse history on measures of PTSD, general stress symptomology, relationship quality, and perceived behaviors in couple interactions. Of these, only the measure of PTSD symptoms reflected significantly higher scores for male partners in the CSA group versus those in the clinical control group. These findings seem to imply that a secondary traumatic stress model may be useful in terms of understanding male partners of childhood sexual abuse survivors, in contrast to the findings of Burgoff (1993) and Ferguson (1993) suggesting more diffuse responses to the abuse for these individuals that are not clearly reflected in existing measures or models of stress. Given these considerations, continued data-driven descriptive study of various responses to trauma that may be more specific to the experiences of male partners of female childhood sexual abuse survivors is clearly warranted.

Chapter 4

METHOD

PARTICIPANTS

Six couples were identified for participation using a purposive sampling method based on the following inclusion criteria: (a) one female member of the couple reported a history of childhood sexual abuse (i.e., the primary survivor), (b) the other member of the couple (i.e., the secondary survivor) denied a personal history of sexual abuse, (c) the couple had been in a relationship for at least 6 months (d) the childhood sexual abuse had already been disclosed to the secondary survivor prior to study participation, and (e) both members of the couple were available and willing to be interviewed about their perceptions of the effects of the abuse on each of them.

Recruitment of participants continued throughout the study, and was discontinued after analysis of the data provided by the sixth couple. This couple added only 13 new themes overall, many of which appeared to be related to their unique issues as the only participating lesbian couple. Specifically, couple six contributed at most one or two new themes to each area of inquiry, with the exception of sexuality, to which they collectively added four themes, and thus saturation of themes was approached or achieved. The decision to discontinue data collection at that juncture also is consistent with the recommendations of Lincoln and Guba (1985) indicating that up to one dozen interviews typically are sufficient to exhaust most available information and yet avoid redundancy. With the six participating couples, the present study generated twelve sets of data relevant to the perceived effects of the abuse for primary and secondary survivors. This chapter focuses exclusively on sequelae for secondary survivors.

Table 1. Demographic Comparison of Participating Couples

Characteristic	Couple					
	1	2	3	4	5	6[a]
	Kelly/Brian	Sally/Fred	Lisa/Stuart	Patty/Ted	Jill/Russ	Pam/Angie
Current Age						
Primary survivor	24	19	25	22	22	20
Secondary survivor	27	27	22	25	25	24
Race/Ethnicity						
Primary survivor	Eur-Amer	Eur-Amer	Eur-Amer	Eur-Amer	Eur-Amer	Eur-Amer
Secondary survivor	Eur-Amer	Eur-Amer	Eur-Amer	Kor-Amer	Eur-Amer	Eur-Amer
Age at onset of abuse (years)	<5	5	4	4	5	9
Relationship duration (years)	8.5	1	2.5	.67	7	.5
Relationship status (married, cohabitating, dating)	M	D	C/D	D	D	C
Time since disclosure (months)	54-64	3	24	5	24-36	5
Relationship intact?	Yes	Yes	No	Yes	No	Yes
Incest?	No	Yes[b]	Yes	Yes[b]	Yes	Yes
Sexual abuse ongoing?	Yes	Yes	Yes	Yes	No	Yes
Concurrent physical abuse or neglect?	No	Yes	No	Yes	No	No

[a]The primary survivor in this couple self-identified as lesbian and the secondary survivor as bisexual. All other couples reported being heterosexual. [b]These primary survivors reported parental incest.

Of the participants, four received written information about the study from their therapists at a Mid-Atlantic university counseling center and volunteered to participate along with their current relationship partners. One couple was referred by another participant in the study, and one couple responded to an invitation for extra credit in an introductory-level psychology course. Although written notices about the research were posted in a community trauma counseling center, no participants presented from that site. Three additional individuals inquired about the study, but one of these couples did not meet the inclusion criteria and two chose not to pursue participation for unspecified reasons. Demographic information pertaining to the final sample is presented in table 1.

MATERIALS

Interview Protocol

Semi-structured interviews were initially developed on the basis of existing literature regarding the adult effects of childhood sexual abuse. Questions were pilot-tested during four analog interviews with individuals who did not meet any of the criteria for study participation, but responded as they believed the participants might and provided feedback about the questions. The questions also were revised throughout the study to include important domains of experience emerging from the ongoing analysis of data.

Specifically, the interviews began with an open-ended question asking the primary survivor to describe the perceived effects of her childhood sexual abuse on herself and on her partner as a secondary survivor. Similarly, the secondary survivor was asked to describe the perceived effects of the primary survivor's childhood sexual abuse on her, and on him- or herself as a secondary survivor. Each participant also was asked to provide an assessment of the nature and extent of his or her awareness regarding effects on the partner, as well as the extent of the partner's awareness regarding effects on the participant. Although the latter is not the focus of this chapter, a description of couples' reciprocal awareness of the adult sequelae of childhood sexual abuse, and the implications of this awareness for conjoint therapy, can be found in Wiersma (2003).

If the interviewee did not spontaneously report any themes from one or more of the major domains reported by other participants in the study, then the interviewee was prompted to indicate whether or not any effects could be noted for self or partner within those domains. The interview concluded with some questions about abuse history and demographic information. Beyond the interview questions, the researcher's remarks consisted primarily of supportive listening responses.

PROCEDURE

Interviews

Interviews varied from 1 hr 45 min to 2 hr 15 min duration and were held in the researcher's office in a counseling center. The primary and secondary survivors were interviewed separately by the researcher, in counterbalanced order.

Because members of each couple were interviewed within a 1-week time frame of each other, the second member of the pair to be interviewed was asked to describe the extent, nature, and influence of any discussions about the abuse or the research with his or her partner during the intervening interval. All participants reported that these discussions were minimal. Referral resources were provided to each participant at the end of each interview and during a 2-week follow-up telephone contact.

Qualitative Analysis

Audiotapes of the interviews were transcribed by the researcher following each interview, and ultimately yielded 365 typed pages of raw data. Likewise, data analysis began after the first interview and was ongoing throughout the data collection phase in order to refine the interview and facilitate the testing of ideas. Specifically, data were coded and analyzed using the open, axial, and selective coding procedures of Strauss and Corbin's (1990) grounded theory method.

Open coding consisted of a line-by-line analysis of the transcripts, during which conceptual working labels were applied to phenomena that were frequently reported and/or that were reported with great intensity. These emergent themes capture the perceived effects of the abuse. Different individual themes also clustered together to comprise several superordinate categories representing different domains of experience perceived to be affected by the abuse (i.e., affective, cognitive, self-perceptual, somatic, sexual, academic- and career-related, and social domains). A simultaneous axial coding process examined relationships among themes, and key antecedents, consequents, contexts, or interactions of the themes were recorded whenever possible. A selective coding process resulted in a descriptive narrative of potential barriers to and facilitators of awareness within couples (Wiersma, 2003).

Four resultant sets of themes describe the perceived sequelae of the primary survivor's childhood sexual abuse (a) for the primary survivor according to her own self-report (b) for the primary survivor as perceived by her partner (c) for the secondary survivor according to his or her own self-report and (d) for the secondary survivor as perceived by his or her partner. The present chapter focuses on the perceived effects for secondary survivors (for a description of perceived effects on the primary survivor or on mutual awareness of these effects, see Wiersma, 1999 and Wiersma, 2003, respectively).

Validity

In keeping with the importance of establishing the "truth value" (Lincoln and Guba, 1985, p. 290) of qualitative research findings, the present study included several measures to demonstrate validity. First, the researcher maintained a journal describing the methodology and its rationale, brief narrative summaries of the contacts with participants, and personal responses to the interviews and data. Second, the design incorporated a triangulation strategy, relying on several different couples, a diverse sample, and input from both primary and secondary survivors in order to gain multiple perspectives on the phenomenon of interest (Lincoln and Guba, 1985; Marshall and Rossman, 1995). Finally, as recommended by Hill and colleagues (Hill et al., 1997), an independent auditor provided oral and written feedback to the researcher at several intervals during the course of the study. Specifically, this auditor was assigned to review the researcher's journal, to trace final themes to their original sources in the transcripts, to review conceptual labels assigned to the themes, to review placement of themes into higher order domains/categories, and to search for negative instances in the data.

Chapter 5

RESULTS

Results consisted of a set of themes descriptive of the sequelae of the primary survivor's childhood sexual abuse for the secondary survivor as perceived by both members of each couple. Specifically, themes derived from both primary and secondary survivors' reports of the affective, cognitive, self-perceptual, somatic, sexual, academic/career, and social sequelae for secondary survivors attributed to the primary survivor's abuse. As suggested Hill, Thompson, and Williams (1997), themes are presented as either general (pertinent to all cases), typical (pertinent to 3, 4, or 5 cases), or variant (pertinent to 1 or 2 cases). Although secondary and primary survivors sometimes differed in the number and nature of themes offered to describe the sequelae of the childhood sexual abuse for the secondary survivors, every effort has been made to present the most frequently reported themes within each domain first, followed by less typical or variant effects. In keeping with the premises of qualitative research, direct quotes of the participants are also included when useful for capturing their subjective experiences of these complex phenomena. Throughout, the term "abuse" is used to refer to the primary survivor's experience of childhood sexual abuse, and the terms "sequel" and "sequelae" to the abuse are used to refer to phenomena experienced by the secondary survivor in the wake of the primary survivor's childhood sexual abuse.

AFFECTIVE SEQUELAE FOR PARTNERS AS SECONDARY SURVIVORS OF CHILDHOOD SEXUAL ABUSE

The affective sequelae of childhood sexual abuse as expressed by participants included a variety of phenomena pertaining to feelings, affective states, and emotional responses. Affective responses that pertained primarily to another domain of experience were included under the more specific domain (e.g., feelings of sexual frustration were included under the sexual domain). Secondary survivors' descriptions of the affective consequences that they have experienced as a result of the primary survivors' abuse yielded a total of 14 themes, with each secondary survivor reporting between three and seven themes. Primary survivors identified 8 themes concerning the affective responses of their partners to the primary survivors' abuse, with the number of such themes ranging from one to five. All primary and secondary survivors addressed the affective domain when discussing sequelae of the abuse for secondary survivors without prompting by the interviewer.

"Bottling up" Feelings

The theme of bottling up feelings was characterized by an effortful tendency by secondary survivors to try to suppress their own feelings about the abuse. This was a general affective sequel to the abuse as reported by all secondary survivors. In addition, all secondary survivors reported bottling up their feelings because they anticipated distress on the part of the primary survivor if she were to be exposed to these emotions. Secondary survivors thereby sought to avoid expressing their feelings about the abuse, articulating that they were doing so largely for the sake of the primary survivor rather than from any personal reluctance to deal with their emotions.

For example, Brian, indicated, "I don't bring it up because I know it bothers her." Fred likewise reported, "The abuse...has such anger in her that...I have to be extra calm and extra careful...with how I act and what I say because of it," and Angie noted, "I try to keep the anger in, 'cause I didn't want her to see the anger, 'cause I didn't want her to think that I was in any way upset with her." Russ also cited his belief that expression of his emotions during relationship conflict related to the abuse would be unproductive: "The angrier I get, probably the less I speak, I would say. Because I just sit there and listen to whoever's mad...rather than...try to discuss it with someone...obviously angry also."

Showing some reluctance to deal with his own feelings as well as those of the primary survivor, Stuart further linked the theme of bottling up feelings with the comparable cognitive phenomenon of blocking thoughts of the abuse, stating, "I didn't feel it was really my place to talk about it....I didn't want to...bring up no bad feelings...or think about it." Ted also evidenced a theme of bottling up his feelings in anticipation of survivor distress, but to a lesser degree:

> It probably would be better if eventually we talked about that....Just so I don't have to hide what I'm feeling....I think it would help her be more comfortable if I could say, "Well, you know, I'm feeling this way. I don't even know if I would call it hiding, because it's such a small part." (Ted)

The tendency of secondary survivors to contain their feelings was also noted as a typical affective sequel to the abuse for secondary survivors as reported by four primary survivors (Kelly, Patty, Jill, and Pam). As phrased by Kelly, "It's not something we really talk about. I think it's because it's so touchy, and he knows that it sets me off. It makes me feel so bad [emphasis]" and by Pam, "We don't talk about this sort of thing....I think it's just because she's afraid she'll say something...to upset me." Patty also appeared to speculate as to whether Ted could be bottling up his feelings and to assess the desirability of such a response:

> He doesn't show...that it bothers him or anything....You know, if it did, I would only wish that he would say something. I don't want him to be...scared to say it. Because...I feel fragile...but I don't want that to...make him scared to tell me how he really feels either. (Patty)

Here, Patty's comment highlights the possibility that at times the secondary survivor may withhold his/her feelings about the abuse on the basis of an untested assumption that the primary survivor would indeed be upset or that it would be better for her not to be upset. In a slightly different variation, Jill described Russ bottling up feelings as a result of his attempts to distance himself from the relationship and its difficulties related to the abuse:

> I had always been able to draw that [emotion] out of him easily, and this time he was putting up a wall, big time....and even though I knew it was there...and he would let it out at certain times, he was being a lot harder about it over the summer. (Jill)

Although two other primary survivors, Sally and Lisa, noted that their partners tend to bottle up their feelings, they attributed this more to the partners' own difficulties with emotional intimacy unrelated to the abuse per se. For example, Sally voiced, "He's the type of person that holds everything in" and "Sometimes he seems to admit feelings that may not really be there. They're just the safest ones or something." Likewise, Lisa did not attribute Stuart's reticence to share emotions to her abuse, but merely to his personality:

> He is not really...a very communicative person. So I've kinda had to read into a lot of things....He never talks about anything....We have to have giant arguments in order for him to even tell me he's feeling bad. (Lisa)

Anger/Hatred

The theme of anger/hatred reflected strong negative affect by the secondary survivor toward the perpetrator, in most cases, and toward the victim, in some cases. This strong negative emotion constituted a general affective sequel to the abuse as referenced by all secondary survivors. For example, Angie noted, "I was angry at her [Pam's] brother and just that it happened. Just anger---" and went on to describe her efforts to contain her anger when with the primary survivor. For Brian, anger at the perpetrator was associated with a cognitive theme of revenge fantasies that he has sometimes disclosed to the primary survivor. In addition to some anger at the perpetrator ("So usually...when we talk about him, I'm usually--sometimes I get a little angry about it"), Fred acknowledged feeling anger at times toward the primary survivor in response to her sexual difficulties ("Sometimes I get mad...I've gotten mad over it because I don't understand it"). Russ also described anger directed at the primary survivor and her abuse-related mistrust ("Like if I want to go out with my friends...like that would get her [Jill} mad, and that would in turn get me angry with her").

For all primary survivors with the exception of Patty, the theme of anger/hatred was cited as a typical sequel to the abuse for secondary survivors. Three of these primary survivors (Sally, Lisa, Jill) indicated that they felt they were the primary recipients of the secondary survivor's anger during relationship conflict that they attributed at least in part to the abuse. For example, Sally voiced, "You'd think...it's [anger is] going towards my dad, but it just...seemed like it was going towards me because he [Fred] didn't want to hear how I felt about it." Lisa also stated, "He [Stuart] was like, 'Well, maybe they all found out what a slut you used to be.' And I was like...well, O.K., there's spite talking." In direct contrast to

Stuart's report, Lisa also discussed an absence of anger on his part toward the perpetrator:

> When we went up there [to see the perpetrators], he [Stuart] knew....And there was nothing [emphasis], you know. If he thought about it or...if he thought anything or if he felt any way, he...never said anything about it....Even sat down and had a big long conversation with the oldest one. (Lisa)

Initial report of few affective sequelae. A typical response by four secondary survivors (Brian, Stuart, Ted, Russ) was to indicate to the interviewer that they had experienced few emotional sequelae in the wake of their partners' childhood sexual abuse ("Pretty much I have the same feelings I did before"--Stuart). Nonetheless, several of these participants went on to describe substantive effects (i.e., eight for Brian, six for Stuart, six for Russ, but only three for Ted) in this domain. In general, Brian's statements appeared to account for his report of experiencing little emotional effect by linking this with the affective theme of bottling up feelings and the cognitive theme of blocking thoughts of the primary survivor's abuse. For example, he stated, "It doesn't affect me at all....Oh, it makes me feel bad, but what are you gonna do? I try not to dwell on it. No use to" and also, "It bothers me when I think about it. I try not to think about it."

Three primary survivors (Kelly, Sally, Patty) also indicated few emotional sequelae to the abuse for their partners. Of these, Kelly stated that there was little emotional effect on Brian, but nonetheless went on to offer five affective themes. Sally reported that the abuse has had a questionable emotional effect on Fred, and appeared to question why he wasn't affected more in that regard: "Things about myself that he should want to, you'd think he would want to hear, be interested in hearing, he is dating me...he will change the subject on me, or...act bored or uninterested." Finally, Patty was in agreement regarding Ted's general assertion that he experienced little emotional impact as a result of her abuse, stating, "I just--I don't know. I don't think it's been a negative."

Impatience Regarding Healing Process

Impatience regarding the duration of the primary survivor's healing process was a typical affective sequel to the abuse presented by five secondary survivors (Brian, Fred, Stuart, Ted, Angie). For several secondary survivors, as detailed by Brian, the impatience was pursuant to a perceived inability to help the primary survivor in her healing and adjustment process:

> I have nothing else to say to her about it....When she starts on that I'll just--What do you do? What do you say?....I've told her that I just feel like making me a sign and just putting it on my shirt and just holding it. (Brian)

Brian further indicated, "Down the road if she's still bawling about it every time it's mentioned, I might go do it [confront perpetrator]." Similarly, Ted noted some small degree of impatience regarding Patty's healing process, stating, "I thought maybe it would lessen, but...ya know, it's not really a big deal really" and also, "I would just think that she would be comfortable around me....because we've been intimate for so long."

Such impatience regarding the healing process was also a variant affective sequel to the abuse as presented by two primary survivors (Kelly, Sally). Kelly reiterated Brian's impatience, expressing, "Sometimes I don't think he understands...the fact that you just don't forget about it....It's not just buried in the backyard and it's not just something that you don't think about anymore." This sentiment was reinforced by Sally, who indicated, "It was weird because it's like he's [Fred is] wanting to close it. Taking him [the perpetrator] to court, he goes to jail...it's done with. And that's not how it works" and also, "He just wants to fix it and be over it."

Loss

This theme was characterized by negative affect most aptly described as sadness, hurt, or woundedness, in other words: a sense of loss. It was a typical affective sequel to the abuse noted by three secondary survivors (Fred, Stuart, Russ). In particular, Stuart outlined a theme of sadness in the context of sexual difficulties and the altered course of his relationship with the primary survivor from the more permanent and committed relationship it might otherwise have been. In a similar fashion, Fred reported feeling hurt as a result of Sally's abuse-related distraction and mistrust of him. In a slightly different context, Russ presented a theme of irrevocable sadness upon hearing Jill's disclosure of her abuse.

The theme of loss was also a typical sequel to the abuse articulated by three primary survivors (Kelly, Jill, Pam). Beyond the affective themes presented by Brian, Kelly referenced his sadness upon her initial disclosure of the abuse, indicating that Brian cried on that occasion. Pam described sadness on the part of Angie, noted nonverbally, in the context of Pam's distancing, stating, "She just gives me the saddest looks...just like, 'How could you possibly not love me as much as I love you?' looks." Quite similarly, Jill noted the hurt inflicted on Russ as a result of her abuse-related mistrust and infidelity, referring to "all the times he would let himself be hurt over and over." Although Lisa relayed a theme of depression on the part of Stuart, she indicated that she believed this was not influenced by her experience of abuse.

Frustration (Non-sexual)

This theme reflected feelings of frustration regarding one's perceived inability to understand and/or assist the primary survivor in her healing and adjustment process, and was presented as a typical affective sequel to the abuse by four secondary survivors (Brian, Fred, Russ, Angie). For example, Russ stated, "It's frustrating, just because it's felt like...no matter what I did or who I was, it wouldn't...compensate for any of that [the abuse]," and Angie noted, "She [Pam] doesn't want me to help her, and so that's been hard for me..." Frustration was also a variant affective sequel to the abuse presented by one primary survivor (Jill). Specifically, Jill noted frustration for Russ related to his perceived inability to make sense of her abuse:

> That had to be really frustrating for him...at least as frustrating as it was for me. Especially not knowing what it's like to be sexually abused...especially not knowing what it's like to feel any of these things. (Jill)

Although Sally made reference to Fred's frustration, she restricted this solely to the sexual realm.

Hope

This theme captured a positive outlook and confidence, in varying degrees, among secondary survivors that the primary survivor would experience healing and that their relationship would consequently improve. This was a typical affective sequel to the abuse indicated by three of the six secondary survivors (Brian, Stuart, Russ). For example, in a manner that would seem to counterbalance his impatience regarding Kelly's healing process, Brian indicated, "she'll work it out when the time comes." Stuart articulated a pattern of themes involving past hope regarding Lisa's healing and adjustment process, related to themes of impatience and then disappointment in this regard, stating, "I figured like later on it would be better, because therapy is not a one day thing [laughs], so I accepted that, but....I was thinking a couple of years, probably" and "It's never really got any better." For Stuart, this decline in hope appeared to be further related to the change in the status of his relationship with the primary survivor, in that they no longer intend to marry.

Relief

Rather than positive affect per se, this theme appeared to capture more of a reprieve from negative affect or distress for secondary survivors. Relief was a typical affective sequel to the abuse as presented by three secondary survivors (Brian, Stuart, Russ), but was not referenced by any primary survivors (in fact, it is interesting to note that primary survivors did not acknowledge *any* positive emotional sequelae of the abuse for their partners). For Brian, such feelings of relief were associated with the idea that the abuse experienced by Kelly was not "worse." In addition, Brian reported relief from distress following successful attempts to help the primary survivor, indicating "It makes me feel better." Finally, Stuart referenced a theme involving some positive feelings of relief in the context of the primary survivor's disclosure of abuse and a resultant decrease in his self-blame for sexual problems in the relationship.

General Distress

This theme pertained to a negative affective state of an unspecified type and was a variant affective sequel to the abuse presented by Couple 1, Brian and Kelly. Brian reported general distress in synchrony with distress experienced by the primary survivor, stating, "It bothers me when she gets worked up about it, but other than that it's the last thing on my mind." Kelly likewise manifested agreement for this theme.

Jealousy

Jealousy constituted a variant affective sequel to the abuse cited by Couple 6, Angie and Pam. Specifically, Angie's jealousy focused on the primary survivor's seeking assistance in healing from the abuse outside the relationship from another primary survivor. As Angie related:

'cause we have a mutual friend and...she goes and talks to her....And so it's been hard for me just to step back and let her...go through this...with somebody else. That's really hard for me. (Angie)

Pam likewise noted the theme of jealousy for Angie, indicating, "She doesn't want to share me with anybody [laughs]," but did not directly apply this to the fact that she is discussing her abuse with another survivor rather than her partner.

Disappointment

Disappointment was a variant affective sequel to the abuse reported by Stuart. In particular, Stuart reported experiencing disappointment regarding the perceived limited extent of the primary survivor's healing and limited improvement in their relationship ("It never really got any better"). This theme was related subsequent to the affective themes of hope and then of impatience regarding the healing process. Whereas Lisa noted a theme of disappointment for Stuart, she restricted this to a sexual context.

Gratitude

A variant affective sequel to the abuse presented by Russ as a secondary survivor, who indicated positive affect in the form of appreciation regarding his own childhood and upbringing ("I guess it made me feel pretty lucky...that I didn't have to go through the same thing myself").

Fear

The theme of fear, in this case fears that the worst of the abuse has not yet been disclosed, was a variant affective sequel to the abuse alluded to by Fred as a secondary survivor. Specifically, Fred indicated:

I feel that there could be [more], you know what I mean, because of the way she [Sally] told me about it in the first place. You know, first she told me about it happened, and it took a long time before she would tell me who it was, and she's always told me that there was [sic] things that if she told me about...that she's done in her past, I wouldn't like her or what not....She's told me that, so it just makes me think, you know, gosh, has she done anything else, or has more happened to her...? (Fred)

Mixed Emotions

Feelings of ambiguity and a divided will were alluded to as a variant affective sequel to the abuse by Angie as a secondary survivor. Specifically, she outlined a dilemma in which she struggled with her emotions regarding the primary survivor seeking help for her recovery outside of their relationship: "I was jealous of that time, but...I understood it, and I thought it was a good thing that she continue to talk to [her friend]."

COGNITIVE SEQUELAE FOR PARTNERS AS SECONDARY SURVIVORS OF CHILDHOOD SEXUAL ABUSE

The cognitive sequelae of childhood sexual abuse, derived from participants' descriptions of their experiences, included themes pertaining to such things as thought processes, knowledge, perceptions, and beliefs. Cognitive responses that pertained primarily to another domain of experience were included under the more specific domain (e.g., change in thoughts about others was included under the social domain).

Overall, secondary survivors generated a total of 15 themes pertaining to their cognitive experience in the wake of their partners' abuse histories. The number of themes generated by individual secondary survivors ranged from 5 to 11. Similarly, their partners reported a total of 10 themes when discussing cognitive effects on their partners as a result of the primary survivors' abuse. The number of such themes noted by individual primary survivors ranged from three to nine. All secondary and primary survivors referred to some cognitive themes without benefit of prompting and, in marked contrast to several other domains, neither secondary nor primary survivors reported that the abuse had little cognitive effect on the secondary survivor.

Attempts to Make Sense of Primary Surviv*or's* Abuse and/or its Sequelae

This theme represented efforts by secondary survivors, both successful and unsuccessful, to figure out how the abuse has influenced the primary survivor and/or their relationship. It also subsumes their attempts to grapple with the reasons for abuse in a more existential fashion. Taken together, this was a very prominent, general cognitive sequel to the abuse as reported by all secondary and primary survivors. Illustrative of this theme, Angie stated, "I'm a 'why' person a lot, like, 'Well, why? What? And what's that?" Likewise, Brian reported successful attempts to discern Kelly's likely mood in relation to her abuse, stipulating, "Oh yes. Yes, sir. Oh yeah, I have it all figured out....I can just, I don't know, just after a while you get a sense for it, you know? You get a gut instinct." Both Fred and Russ noted the important role of the primary survivors' disclosures about the abuse in contributing to some success in understanding the primary survivor:

> I was starting to connect the abuse to...what was going on....It was like "Oh"...about her getting angry all the time....I just started basically just linking...some of the things she was doing to that [the abuse]. (Fred)

And likewise:

> We've gone out for a long time, like almost 7 years, and in the beginning, I think she acted sort of the same way, but I didn't know....I didn't know any of the things about her past or anything, so I didn't know why she might have been acting that way. And eventually I think that...kind of just once she told me, that kind of made more things come into focus as to why she acted the way she did before. (Russ)

Angie (as with primary survivor Jill) also made reference to making sense of the abuse during the course of the interview process, connecting the abuse with the nature of Pam's interactions with her family of origin and with Pam's discomfort at being touched, and indicating, "That's probably why....I never thought about it that way."

Attempts to make sense of abuse sequelae for the primary survivor that were perceived by the secondary survivors to be unsuccessful were also prominent, as indicated by Fred:

I've thought about that, and I haven't really been able to put anything together about what I would think about that....I've thought about it and I don't really know why it's like that. (Fred)

In a related fashion, unsuccessful attempts to reconcile within one's self how something like child sexual abuse could actually take place were reported by both Stuart ("I didn't really understand why something like that would happen" and Ted ("I just don't understand it, and why it happens...").

For primary survivors Kelly and Patty, their partners' attempts to make sense of the ramifications of the abuse were perceived as desirable and as largely successful. For instance, with respect to the role of her abuse in her thinking processes, Kelly stated, "I think he's [Brian's] very aware of it....he knows how much I think about it, and how big a part it [the abuse] probably plays." Pam, however, gave some indication that she felt threatened by Angie's attempts to make sense of the abuse, noting, "That's just another part of her trying to...cross that line or, I don't know, find out things that I just don't want her to know yet, maybe."

Questioning Role of Primary Survivor's Abuse in Observed Difficulties

In a related theme, participants also described some confusion regarding whether or not the primary survivor's experience of abuse has contributed to personal problems of either partner or to their relationship problems, and if so to what extent. This was a general cognitive sequel to the abuse as reported by secondary survivors. Brian, for instance, referred to questioning the role of the abuse in Kelly's difficulties:

I think a lot of it's just the pressure from school, too. So that's what I'm saying. It's not solely--I can't blame it all on that [the abuse]. I know they're intertwined.... I can't really separate them out. Sometimes I can, but not always. So it's not fair for me to blame it all on her [abuse] experience. (Brian)

As did Russ:

Like I told you that her parents got divorced. And I like felt that that was such a big part of it...because she didn't seem to really remember much of the whole abuse incident....like I thought she just had an anti-male thing because of her dad....So I guess I still, even though I found out about that [the abuse], I guess I still attributed most of it to the whole divorce issue rather than just the sexual abuse. (Russ)

Similarly, Angie speculated about the role of the abuse during the interview ("I don't know if this has anything to do with the abuse but...") and wondered about its influence on Pam's fear of abandonment, their mutual weight gain, and her own perceived pattern of self-sacrifice in the relationship.

Questions among secondary survivors about the role of the primary survivor's abuse in contributing to personal or relationship problems were also described as a typical sequel to the abuse as reported by three primary survivors (Sally, Lisa, Jill). As did Brian, Kelly made reference to his confusion regarding "...the impact that that [the abuse] can have on different areas..." Unlike Ted, Patty did not note any confusion on his part regarding the role of the abuse in observed problems but expressed that he is "very aware...'cause...a lot of reactions that I have will happen...I mean, it's obvious what's setting it off." In a further related dynamic, Sally described Fred as uncritically relating all problems to the abuse rather than questioning its contribution, indicating, "He personally thinks, if you ask him, that my whole personality is due to that [the abuse]. I don't think it is. I think it's a mixture of everything but...he thinks my whole attitude."

Intrusive Thoughts of Primary Survivor's Abuse

Experiencing unwanted and/or repeated thoughts about the primary survivor's experience of abuse was a typical cognitive sequel to the abuse as suggested by all secondary survivors with the exception of Russ. Brian, for example, noted, "It bothers me when I find myself thinking about it. I try not to think about it." Intrusive thoughts of the abuse for secondary survivors were likewise reported by three primary survivors (Kelly, Sally, Pam). For a number of secondary and primary survivors, this theme was associated with a further related theme of attempting to avoid or dispel such thoughts.

Blocking Thoughts of Primary Survivor's Abuse

Effortful attempts to block intrusive thoughts of the abuse were reported as a typical cognitive sequel to the abuse by four secondary (Brian, Stuart, Ted, Angie) survivors, and were associated with the companion theme of bottling up feelings in the affective domain. As Brian emphasized, "I try not to dwell on it. No use to....I just try to block it out" and, when queried, indicated "Just don't think about it, you know [laughs]? I just, "O.K. Forget about it. I'll think about something else. I have a lot of self-control. I do. I have a lot of discipline."

A similar pattern was reported by Stuart:

> I just wanted to stop thinking about it, so I'd start thinking about something else. Something easier to think about....Just switch gears. Start thinking about homework or something. Watch T.V. Go somewhere....It usually worked pretty good. Just think about different things. (Stuart)

And this phenomenon was also observed for Ted ("I never dwell on it...") and for Angie ("I don't let myself think about it often. I'm like, 'Oh, it's all right. If she's happy, I'm happy"). Although Russ stated that he did not experience thoughts of the childhood sexual abuse during sexual activity, he did not attribute this to a deliberate attempt to block his thoughts or not to think about the abuse as did the other secondary survivors. Blocking thoughts of the abuse was likewise reported for secondary survivors by three of their partners (Kelly, Sally, Pam).

"Thinking Twice" in Interactions with Primary Survivor

Using caution and hesitating in order to think through how the primary survivor may respond to abuse-related stimuli or disclosures was described as a quite typical cognitive sequel to the abuse by all secondary survivors with the exception of Russ. For secondary survivors, this reliance on forethought was unilaterally presented as associated with their attempts to avoid creating any distress that might be anticipated in the primary survivor. For example, Brian stated, "I have made a couple of mistakes and said things that led to it [discussion of the abuse]" and "I try to think before I speak now [laughs]. A little more so, you know?" Likewise, Ted indicated a theme of employing forethought to avoid anticipated distress of the primary survivor, stating, "Sometimes if I'm not...if I don't think about it, it, sometimes my reaction--it's like "What are you doing?"". Angie also voiced a theme of employing forethought to avoid anticipated distress of the primary survivor, noting that this is "hard to gauge" due to the variability in Pam's emotional and sexual response. This same theme was presented as a variant sequel to the abuse as reported by two primary survivors (Kelly, Patty). Kelly noted, "He's more careful about...bringing even things maybe up [sic] that are of that nature to begin with" and Patty was also in agreement regarding this response by Ted, but only as pertains to the sexual realm.

Increased General Knowledge Regarding Childhood Sexual Abuse

As a typical cognitive sequel to the abuse, five primary survivors (Kelly, Sally, Patty, Jill, Pam) indicated the belief that their partners had acquired a greater understanding of the issue of childhood sexual abuse in general as a result of their affiliation with the primary survivors. Sally, for instance, said, "He's [Fred is] understanding more...that it does affect girls..." Both Sally and Pam went on to acknowledge that there was room for further growth in this area, in that their partners continued to misunderstand much about abuse and its effects (see the theme regarding lack of understanding, below).

This assessment that their general knowledge about sexual abuse has increased as a result of their partners' experiences was also a variant cognitive sequel to the abuse as reported by two secondary survivors (Stuart, Russ). In this respect, Stuart discussed his insight "that it [abuse] was as prevalent as it was and...just the different things that are considered sexual abuse." Russ also noted that his awareness of abuse had increased, and yet described this as "a real superficial knowledge of stuff like that" and expressed a desire for even more information (see below).

Loss of Naiveté

A change in worldview characterized by a kind of loss of innocence when confronting painful realities, such as abuse, was reported as a typical cognitive sequel to the abuse as reported by three secondary (Stuart, Ted, Russ) survivors. This was captured best by Russ, who voiced, "Nothing bad happened when I was a kid....And then to think that, o.k., this might happen...that it does happen, and you go on thinking, o.k., this might happen again" and also, "Not really like a loss of innocence, I guess, but all the same, maybe, kind of." A similar loss was alluded to by Stuart ("It opened my eyes more...") and by Ted:

> It's kinda boggling, mind-boggling that that goes on.... I don't know if that's because of Patty. I mean, that could be because of anybody. But because we're close, you know, it's someone I know, then it's even more sort of, I don't know if shocking is the word. (Ted)

A loss of naiveté in the secondary survivor was also noted by three of their partners (Kelly, Lisa, Jill), including Lisa who observed, "Now he [Stuart] can see that people do have their little Achille's heels."

Curiosity Regarding Primary Survivor's Abuse

Wondering about and wanting to know more about the primary survivor's experience of abuse and/or abuse sequelae was a typical cognitive sequel to the abuse as reported by four secondary survivors (Brian, Fred, Stuart, Angie). This "interest" (Brian) was expanded by Fred who indicated, "I kept pickin' her brain at it here and there whenever the time was right to...just ask about it [the abuse events], 'cause I was curious, you know?" Angie also referenced this theme of curiosity ("I'm nosey"), which contributed to the universally presented themes of attempts to make sense of the sexual abuse as well as questioning the role of the abuse in observed difficulties. This response by secondary survivors remained unacknowledged by primary survivors.

Memory of Primary Survivor's Abuse Disclosure

Statements that they did not remember the primary survivor's initial disclosure of the abuse (Russ) or that they did not remember their response to that disclosure (Brian, Stuart, Ted, Russ) was a typical cognitive sequel to the abuse for secondary survivors. This theme was typified by Russ's statements, "I don't really remember what the conversation was like" and also by that of "I don't really remember how I responded".

Adopting a Critical Stance toward Primary Survivor's Healing Process

This theme pertained to a perception among primary survivors that their partners formed and articulated unfair judgments about the course of their recovery from the abuse. Specifically, this was a typical cognitive sequel to the abuse among secondary survivors as reported by four primary survivors (Kelly, Sally, Lisa, Pam). Expressed Kelly:

He [Brian] was just like, "Really?! You think about that [the abuse] every day?! Why? Why do you think about that every day?"...'Cause I know he...thinks, you know, "That's not productive [imitates stern voice] to think about every day." (Kelly)

And Sally stressed:

I try to tell him..it ain't going to do anybody any good, I personally think, to put him [perpetrator] in jail right now....I personally just think it's more trouble than it's worth. Me going through therapy and going back and facing it personally, that might help, but...he just...was literally arguing with me....He just kept going on and on about this, "Put him in jail, that's what you need to do." And I'm like, "I don't agree with you," and he's like, "No, you're wrong. You need to do this." (Sally)

She continued on to say, "He tries to say, if you ask him his attributes...open-minded would be one of them, but I personally think he's full of it, because he's close-minded." Similarly, Lisa referred to Stuart's criticism of her periodic desire to work through the abuse on her own versus seeing a counselor and Pam noted a theme of a judgmental stance by Angie toward the primary survivor's healing process, as evidenced by Angie's perceived failure to give Pam space. In this regard, Pam indicated, "I don't think she accepts the reasons why I need space and...she doesn't really try to give me that space there [emotionally] as much as sexually" and later, "I think she would kind of think it was bullshit [laughs], you know. Just something for me to say."

Lack of Understanding of Primary Survivor's Abuse

Some degree of failure among secondary survivors to understand the influence of the primary survivor's abuse was reported as a typical cognitive sequel to the abuse by three primary survivors (Kelly, Sally, Pam). This was also an area in which primary survivors seemed conflicted, or at least measured, regarding the extent of the secondary survivors' understanding. For example, in addition to reporting some increased partner knowledge about abuse and its ramifications, Kelly also stated, "Sometimes I don't think he understands..." Similarly, Sally qualified her report of Fred's understanding by adding "but then again I don't think he realizes...how much it does" and Pam reported, "I would think that she [Angie] would understand more than she does. I mean, she understands a lot, probably a lot more than most people would, but it's all sexually." This theme was not directly articulated by any secondary survivors, although Russ did express a desire for even more knowledge about childhood sexual abuse in a general sense.

Revenge Fantasies

Thoughts of exacting revenge on the perpetrator was a further variant cognitive sequel to the abuse reported by two secondary survivors (Brian, Stuart). Brian, in particular, spoke of fantasies about taking "forced vengeance" on the perpetrator:

> I know right where he lives today....If I ever get the chance, I would get into it with him....It's not worth me getting into trouble....I one time asked...our attorney, I told him one time, I said, "If you were gonna go give somebody a good country thrashin', no clubs, knives, guns, nothing', just a good thrashin', and to let him
> know why he's gettin' it", you know? (Brian)

Among primary survivors, Kelly also indicated this response by Brian:

> He [Brian] said..."If I could do it and get away with it, if there's ever a day that... we're still alive and...people are what they describe in the Bible and everything as being the Final Days," he said, "I will kill him [the perpetrator]" He's said many times too..."If I could do it and get away with it, I would....hire some people and have him [the perpetrator] beaten up." (Kelly)

Attempts at Perspective Taking

Trying to adopt the perspective of the primary survivor and imagine what it might be like to be "in her shoes" was described as a variant cognitive sequel to the abuse as reported by secondary survivors, Stuart and Russ. As phrased by Stuart:

> I think it would probably make me feel a little upset [laughs slightly] if that [abuse] happened to me...I just think about how I would feel about it, how I would maybe deal with it....But I tend to do that, too. Put my--think how I would feel in the situation. (Stuart)

Primary survivors did not report this particular theme for their partners.

Change in Beliefs about Criminal Justice System

A variant cognitive sequel to the abuse reported by Stuart as a secondary survivor, this theme articulated a change in belief toward stricter punishment for perpetrators of sexual crimes:

> More of a belief in like...stricter penalties for it....I had always considered it [abuse] bad, so it wasn't like I was thinking it was good and then all the sudden thinking it was bad, but...just more of a belief in punishing the...offender. (Stuart)

A companion theme for Stuart was anger at the perpetrator of the abuse.

Vivid Memories of Primary Survivor's Abuse Disclosure

A very vivid recollection of the primary survivor's initial abuse disclosure was reported by Brian as a variant cognitive sequel to the abuse for himself as a secondary survivor. This theme was described by Brian, accompanied by a related theme addressing a reported lack of memory regarding his response, as he indicated, "I still remember the exact same place I was on the highway driving down the road when we was [sic] dating, whenever she told me." A further companion theme for Brian was that of intrusive thoughts regarding the abuse.

Desire for Increased General Knowledge regarding Childhood Sexual Abuse

As referenced above, a variant cognitive sequel to the abuse was the desire for additional information pertinent to childhood sexual abuse in general, beyond that pertaining to one's own partner in particular. This theme was captured by Russ as a secondary survivor in relation to perceived deficits in the knowledge he has managed to acquire:

> I guess if I knew in general what people went through that had that happen, or not even what they went through, but just how they reacted to it, if there even is some type of typical...progression after that happens. (Russ)

Self-talk as Coping

Attempting to use reassuring self-statements and positive affirmations to deal with the primary survivor's abuse and its ramifications was a further variant theme. This cognitive sequel to the abuse reported by secondary survivor, Angie. Specifically, Angie related:

> Like if I can talk to myself and if I'm O.K., then we're fine....Like I have to tell myself and it doesn't--like that's my worst thing. I don't do very good about talking to myself about this....But like usually I can talk myself into being O.K. (Angie)

And similarly, when prompted, "I think it would surprise her [Pam] that I have to talk to myself all the time."

SELF-PERCEPTUAL SEQUELAE FOR PARTNERS AS SECONDARY SURVIVORS OF CHILDHOOD SEXUAL ABUSE

The self-perceptual sequelae of childhood sexual abuse generated by participants reflected the influence of childhood sexual abuse on such things as their self-esteem, self-efficacy, self-perceptions, and roles, as integral to one's sense of identity. Self-perceptual sequelae that pertained specifically to another identified domain were included in that domain (e.g., low sense of sexual self-efficacy was included in the sexual domain).

Sequelae in the self-perceptual domain for secondary survivors were presented without prompting by all secondary survivors, with the exception of Russ, and all primary survivors. Secondary survivors generated a total of 12 abuse-related themes in this domain descriptive of their own experience. The number of themes articulated by individual secondary survivors ranged from three to nine. Primary survivors presented a total of 12 such themes, with a range of two to seven themes described by each primary survivor.

Adopting Role of Comforter

Attempts to comfort and soothe the primary survivor were a general role adopted in the wake of the abuse according to all participating secondary survivors. There were a variety of strategies for providing comfort, both successful and unsuccessful, mentioned by both secondary and primary survivors. Brian, for example, referred specifically to verbal reassurance ("repeatedly telling her that it's o.k."). Other secondary survivors, such as Angie and Russ, described inefficacious attempts at comforting:

It's not good. It doesn't work out well, like it doesn't balance 'cause...I'm a real huggy person...and so when I try to soothe it's like a touching, like calm voice, you know, "I love you. It's O.K." like a stroking kind of thing. (Angie)

The attempt by secondary survivors to adopt the role of comforter was also a typical response reported by all primary survivors with the exception of Lisa. Specifically, Kelly described the role-related theme of comforter adopted by Brian at the time of her original disclosure of the abuse, stating, "I just remember he comforted me a lot" and "I just remember he put his arm around me and I remember...he cried." The role of physical touch was also reported by Patty:

...And he [Ted] came up here [to counseling center] with me, and he stayed...and like when we left, I walked over there and sat down. He just gave me a big hug. (Patty)

Sally, in contrast, only partially endorsed Fred's role as comforter, suggesting that he does not always execute this role as successfully as he might ("He just kinda set [sic] there and was supportive but there wasn't really anymore conversation between us"). Regarding this lack of verbal reassurance, Patty expressed, "He [Ted] didn't say anything [laughs], he just held me. That's pretty much all he does. I mean, there really isn't anything he can say, anything he can do." In general, Patty seemed more accepting of this response by her partner than did other primary survivors such as Sally or even Lisa, who did not report efforts by Stuart to comfort her, and it is interesting to note that Patty and Ted's relationship is characterized by significantly less conflict than that of Sally and Fred or Lisa and Stuart.

Low Sense of Self-efficacy about Assisting Primary Survivor

Believing that one is not adequate to the task of helping the primary survivor cope with or heal from the abuse was a general and very salient self-perceptual theme presented by all secondary survivors. Interestingly, several instances of low self-efficacy were associated with unsuccessful attempts, either perceived or actual, by the secondary survivor to help the primary survivor. For some secondary survivors, this low self-efficacy was reported in spite of previously successful efforts to help their partners.

General and multiple instances of low self-efficacy with respect to helping were related by Brian: "I've tried to talk about it and I can't," "There's nothing I can do," and "I don't know what to say...I've said all I can say. There's nothing you can say." Fred also noted unsuccessful attempts to help the primary survivor, particularly in the context of her anger:

> Sometimes I feel like no matter what I do for her, it's not gonna be good enough. Like...I could buy her roses every day for a year, but if I stepped on her toe one day, all those roses wouldn't mean anything....I can do good things for her all the time, but she remembers the bad things I do over the good things. (Fred)

On this point, he further noted, "I don't really know what to say to her....I feel like no matter what I say it's gonna be the wrong thing to say." Quite similarly, in the event that Patty should ever decide to further discuss her abuse history with him, Ted related:

> If it would help her to talk to me about it, then that would be great, but...at the same time, it just seems [breaks off]...'cause I don't know how much I could help her....I don't know how to respond to that...if she were to...really start giving me the low down. (Ted)

Ted continued on to report, "I think I would just sort of be overwhelmed....So I wouldn't want that to happen and then...say the wrong thing or not say anything and have her feel like she just made herself vulnerable." On this point, he concluded, "I don't know if I'm the right person."

For Russ, the theme of low self-efficacy in relation to helping the primary survivor seemed to result in a kind of learned helplessness that he perceived as detrimental to intimacy in the relationship. For instance, he indicated:

> It's felt like no matter what I did or who I was, it wouldn't...compensate for any of that [the abuse]....So however I've acted or whatever I've said and did, or however I've treated her, couldn't measure up to what happened to her previously. (Russ)

As a result, Russ implicated the consequent social theme of distancing from the survivor, stating, "I've felt like there's nothing really that I could do to change it, so there are a lot of times that when [sic] I just do not want to be there at all."

Russ also extended the theme of low self-efficacy to a further theme of questioning his capacities as a potential parent.

For Stuart, the theme of low self-efficacy regarding his ability to help the primary survivor, was particularly associated with a tendency to compare his helping efforts to those of a sexual abuse survivor from whom Lisa also receives assistance:

> I'd kinda feel like a third wheel. Just probably be going, "Ooh, that's bad." I mean, I couldn't really do anything....I wouldn't...know what to say, or wouldn't be able to do anything...I think it would be just be better for...those two to talk. (Stuart)

He went on to state, "I would like to, but I don't know how that [sic] I would be able to...just without...going through the experience [of abuse]." Finally, Angie also described low self-efficacy with respect to attempts to help Pam that appeared to contribute to Angie's confusion regarding key aspects of her identity:

> I just feel helpless. I feel like there's not anything that I can do to help her through this, because...she doesn't want me to be the one to help her through it. (Angie)

A low sense of self-efficacy among secondary survivors with respect to their ability to help the primary survivor was also provided as a typical self-perceptual theme by four primary survivors (Sally, Lisa, Patty, Jill). The theme was summarized by Patty, who stated, "He [Ted] doesn't know what to do. He doesn't know what to say." Both Sally and Lisa implied some criticism of their partners' low self-efficacy in this regard, "He's just like, 'Oh, I can't make you happy'" (Sally) and:

> [Abused friend] was like holding me, and he was like, "It's o.k., man. I know exactly what you're going through. I've been there. Just cry. Let it out." But Stuart wasn't like that. Stuart was like, it was like he just...had no idea what to do. He had no idea what to say, to the point that he wouldn't even attempt to do anything about it....like he was just paralyzed. (Lisa)

As a result of this response style these primary survivors appeared to assign their partners the role of custodian rather than that of comforter (see below).

Role of Advisor

Attempting to give advice and to provide wise counsel to the primary survivor was a typical role adopted in the wake of the abuse as perceived by all secondary survivors with the exception of Stuart. For two secondary survivors (Russ, Ted), advice was predominantly geared toward motivating the primary survivor to seek counseling ("I encouraged her to...come here [to counseling]"--Ted). For other secondary survivors, advice-giving centered on particular strategies for healing, including "Why don't you want to talk about it? To me, that would get it out of you and make you feel better" (Brian) and recommendations for the primary survivor to file criminal charges against the perpetrator (Fred).

Secondary survivors adopting the role of advisor was also a variant self-perceptual sequel to the abuse perceived by two primary survivors (Patty, Pam). Patty also implicated an additional role-related theme of advisor:

> I was like..."I guess, you know, I really should [seek counseling]." And [Ted's] like, you know, "I think you should, too." [laughs]

Variants of this role as presented by primary survivors tended to be more negatively framed, and included the role of "preacher" and that of "drill sergeant," as noted below.

Initial Report of Few Self-perceptual Sequelae

A typical response by all secondary survivors with the exception of Angie was to note, initially, that the primary survivor's experience of abuse had not greatly affected the secondary survivors' self-perceptions. Stuart, for example, originally indicated little negative or positive effect on his self-perception related to Lisa's childhood sexual abuse, stating, "I pretty much look at myself in the same way....I don't think it's really changed me very much." However, these secondary survivors (including Stuart) went on to talk about a variety of changes in the way that they see themselves and in the roles that they fill, with individual secondary survivors noting between three and seven themes.

Role of Custodian

In addition to or instead of comforter, the role of custodian was assigned to secondary survivors as a typical role adopted in the wake of the abuse by four primary survivors (Sally, Lisa, Patty, Jill). Sally, for instance, identified Fred's role more as that of custodian than that of comforter as he had reported:

> He's real big on...he helps me out physically, you know. If I need a ride somewhere he helps me or he provides for me here and there or loans me money when I can't. He's like my major support in that way, but when it comes to I have a problem, I go to him, he's more like criticizing the cause of the problem or me for not dealing with it instead of saying, "Well, how do you feel about the problem?" (Sally)

Similarly, in his absence of knowing what else to do, Lisa described Stuart's response as slightly more helpful and primarily custodial in nature. For example, during her bout of depression, she noted, "For two weeks, he was really good, you know, about giving me soup and making me eat, and telling me, 'You have to eat something. Here's some tea....Do you want me to let you have some privacy?'" "Custodian" was also a variant role adopted as perceived by two secondary survivors (Russ, Angie).

Role as Tolerator

In a rather nominal form of supportiveness, finding one's self in a position of "putting up with" or just "getting through" the primary survivor's healing process was a further typical role reported by four secondary survivors (Fred, Ted, Russ, Angie). Fred noted, "I just gotta kind of like go with it" and Ted as tolerator ("I will be tolerant of whatever she has to do"). In an apparently pronounced and pervasive form of this tolerance role, Angie concluded, "I'm just a selfless martyr. God!" This was also recognized as a variant role according to Russ and Angie's partners, Jill (referring to "everything he's [Russ has] put up with") and Pam.

Increased Sense of Self-efficacy

This positive theme consisted of feeling capable at assisting the primary survivor and at other things was a typical sequel to the abuse reported by three secondary survivors (Brian, Fred, Stuart). This theme also appeared to coexist in tension with that of low self-efficacy associated with perceived difficulties assisting the primary survivor, in that both themes were reported by three of the same secondary survivors. As described by Brian:

> These are just the ways that I counteract it [the abuse]. I've tried to build her self-esteem up, and I have a lot [emphasis]. I have built her self-esteem. I would say I've doubled her self-esteem. When I first met her, it was like you would not believe. It was very low. And she'll...tell you. She'll tell me that I have. (Brian)

Further related comments by Brian included "Makes me feel like a success" and "I'm pretty much ready for anything." In addition, Stuart reported enhanced self-efficacy regarding perceived successful outcomes of his role as comforter to the primary survivor, a further related theme:

> I would try to console her and stuff like that....hugging and...trying to talk about it. I guess pretty much just being there, so she said it helped a little bit, I think....It seemed to calm her down a little bit. She wasn't as upset so....it was not difficult. It was really easy. (Stuart)

And expressed more tentatively:

> I think it [the relationship] played a pretty good role in it [Lisa's improvement]. Probably having somebody there to kinda lean on if you needed to, or be there for you. I think that probably had something to do with it. That's wishful thinking too, maybe [laughs]. (Stuart)

Role of Detective

In a companion theme to the cognitive theme of attempts to make sense of the abuse, three secondary survivors (Brian, Fred, Angie) described a typical role adopted in the wake of the abuse that appeared to involve a process of empirical observation and deduction in an effort to detect what is going on with the primary survivor. Offering an example of this role of detective, Angie outlined:

> If [Pam's] on the couch and...she's sitting with an open posture...then it's usually O.K. [to address or touch her], but if she's sittin' towards the end of the couch, like that [crosses arms and legs], then..that's clear that's a time when she wants to be by herself, and if she's moving...she's just moving

around...walking around doing stuff, then that's a time that she doesn't...want to have any close contact. (Angie)

Pam demonstrated agreement for the role-related themes of Angie acting as detective ("She's kinda gettin' under my skin, kinda, and figuring things out").

Self-Defensive Stance

This theme involved adopting a role of defending one's self against abuse-related responses in the primary survivor that were perceived as unjustly directed toward the secondary survivor. This was a variant self-perceptual sequel to the abuse cited by two secondary survivors (Fred, Russ). Specifically, Fred described himself as a defender of his own behavior in the context of feeling "targeted" by Sally's mistrust and anger emanating from the abuse. With respect to this theme, he reported, "I've never lied to her. I've never done anything bad toward her....I don't understand this a lot of times because...she'll say she can't trust me with something even though she has no reason not to." Fred continued, "I feel like that a lot....It seems like every time I have to mention the fact that...'Hey, I've never done anything yet like that...so why are you thinking I would?'"

Role of Preacher

A variant self-perceptual sequel to the abuse that involved a negative slant on the role of advisor was reported by two primary survivors (Sally, Jill). In both of these cases, the primary survivor indicated that, rather than advise, the secondary survivor tries to "lecture" her or tell her what she "should" do in order to recover from her abuse. As a specific example, Jill reported, "He [Russ] would just...be like, 'You need to stop doing that,' or whatever. And I was like, 'Well...Hi! I know that. It's like I just don't...know how.'"

Maintaining a Separate Sense of Self

A variant self-perceptual sequel to the abuse cited by Brian as a secondary survivor was an emphasis on maintaining boundaries and a separate sense of self, although he does not always do so successfully according to Kelly. Specifically, Brian qualified, "Maybe I'm comparing apples to oranges" when comparing himself and his partner, and their respective responses to the abuse. He also asserted, "I have my own thing I'm going towards."

Role of Nurturer

The role of nurturer, noted for the broader, more specific, and mutual reference to "maternal" qualities ("I find her being very motherly towards me"-- Pam) rather than the more limited and specific means of providing comfort cited above, was a variant self-perceptual sequel to the abuse noted by Couple 6, Pam and Angie. In particular, this isolated theme appeared to imply something different, more pro-active and growth-oriented, than mere custodial care. It may also be interesting to note that this maternal framing of the concept of comfort was provided by the only participating couple consisting of two females.

Identity Confusion

The secondary survivor's confusion about important aspects of identity and/or boundaries was a variant self-perceptual sequel to the abuse tentatively alluded to by Couple Six, Angie and Pam. It appeared that, for Angie, a perceived inability to help the primary survivor may contribute to a broader questioning and confusion regarding who she is, what her life is about, or what her role is with respect to her partner:

> I got my undergraduate in psych, and...I'm in grad school now...so I'm all about like wanting to help her...but she doesn't want me to help her. And so that's been hard for me....

and, "I'm a live-to-serve-other-people kind of person, and it feels like there's nothing I can do to ever make her happy." In this regard, Pam tentatively noted Angie's failure to maintain a separate sense of self ("Like there's an Angie, not just Angie-and-Pam"), although she was unsure to what extent this may be related to the childhood sexual abuse.

Role of Drill Sergeant

In a slightly different version of the roles of advisor and preacher, the role of drill sergeant was another variant self-perceptual sequel to the abuse as reported by Kelly as a primary survivor. In this instance, Kelly made reference to Brian's regimented "army or navy person mentality" in relation to her healing process, and reported, "He'll say, 'I've got to make myself do it. You've just got to make yourself do it. You've just got to make yourself do it [repeated like a chant]."

Low Self-esteem

This variant theme, mentioned briefly by Angie as a secondary survivor, appeared to constitute a more globally negative self-assessment than the theme of low self-efficacy solely in assisting the survivor. Specifically, Angie indicated, "I don't feel good about myself when she's sad and there's nothing I can do." This interpretation is strengthened by the use of the emotional language (i.e., "feel") and by the broader apparent questioning of her sense of self as a person (i.e., "huggy," "helping") suggested by Angie.

Role of Strong Survivor

A presentation of strength and invincibility perceived to be adopted by the secondary survivor was a variant self-perceptual sequel to the abuse reported by Kelly for Brian. Specifically, Kelly related, "He's so strong...he doesn't really need me to comfort him because he's so strong by himself."

Role of Therapist

The secondary survivor's attempt to fill the role of the primary survivor's therapist was a variant self-perceptual sequel to the abuse reported by Pam as a primary survivor. Specifically, Pam cited:

> The other day, she brought two books home from the library, and she's like, "I brought you home something that you might want to read." And inside there was some notes that she had written down, like questions she

thinks I should ask myself, and I don't want her to be my...psychiatrist....And that's kinda what she's taking there, kinda put herself right there. (Pam)

Interestingly, in an apparent and appropriate limitation to perceived self-efficacy, two secondary survivors (Brian, Russ) explicitly stated that they could not fill the role of therapist, indicating, "I'm not a psychologist!"

Profound Self-perceptual Sequelae

In a variant sequel to the abuse, Angie was the sole secondary survivor who indicated that there has been a profound effect on her self-perception as a result of her partner's childhood sexual abuse. In this domain, a total of nine self-perceptual themes were noted by Angie with respect to her own experience, six of which were also identified by her partner.

SOMATIC SEQUELAE FOR PARTNERS AS SECONDARY SURVIVORS OF CHILDHOOD SEXUAL ABUSE

The somatic sequelae of childhood sexual abuse for secondary survivors articulated by participants reflected perceived physical symptoms, changes, and physiological states attributed to the primary survivor's experience of childhood sexual abuse. Because of their prominence, responses that were primarily sexual in nature were included in a separate but related domain pertaining to sexual themes. Somatic responses that were part of the diagnostic criteria for depression, anxiety, dissociative, or other non-sexual disorders (e.g., flashbacks, dissociation) were included here.

Only two secondary survivors spontaneously indicated any somatic effect on themselves whatsoever (i.e., alcohol use, gastric distress). When prompted, only one additional instance of a potential somatic effect (i.e., weight gain) was reported, and this remained very tentative in nature. The three remaining secondary survivors indicated that they experienced no somatic effects related to the primary survivor's experience of childhood sexual abuse.

Similarly, primary survivors in the present study did not spontaneously report any somatic responses by their partners related to the childhood sexual abuse. Rather, with two minor exceptions, primary survivors overwhelmingly indicated that there were no somatic effects on their partners stemming from the primary survivors' abuse histories. The two exceptions pertained to the possibility of related weight gain for secondary survivors, and were presented very tentatively by primary survivors as more likely due to a variety of other factors. In one of these instances, the possibility of weight gain indirectly related to the primary survivor's abuse was also tentatively presented by the secondary survivor. It is interesting to note that this instance of agreement concerning weight gain occurred for the sole female secondary survivor represented in the study. As would be expected given the relatively small number of overall perceived somatic sequelae, there were no general somatic sequelae for secondary survivors reported by all primary and/or secondary survivors.

No Somatic Sequelae

As noted above, a typical response by three secondary survivors (Brian, Fred, Ted) was to report that they had not experienced any somatic repercussions of the primary survivor's experience of abuse. A lack of somatic sequelae was also noted by four primary survivors (Kelly, Sally, Patty, Jill). As phrased by Sally, "I don't know if it [the abuse] has affected it [Fred's physical well-being] at all...I just think that maybe a quarter of our problems may be directly related to it [the abuse], or maybe half...but not, not things like that."

Possible Weight Gain

The theme of weight gain by the secondary survivor that might possibly by attributed to abuse-related relationship problems was a variant somatic sequel to the abuse hesitantly presented by one secondary survivor. Specifically, Angie indicated that a causal relationship was unlikely but possible:

> I don't know if...it's probably because we go out to eat all the time and that's why I gain weight, or if it's because...she's upset, so she eats, and I don't want her to eat by herself [so] I eat with her. But that's...that's a reach. (Angie)

This theme was also tentatively reported by two primary survivors (Lisa, Pam). Although not noted by Stuart as a personal somatic response, Lisa clearly questioned whether her childhood sexual abuse might be implicated in Stuart's apparent weight gain:

I don't know if that has anything to do with it, but he did. He put on a lot of weight. More recently. 'Cause we went out, I guess, probably about 9 months before I told him. And then, after that, you know. It was more noticeable more recently. (Lisa)

Similarly, when asked whether Angie experiences any somatic effects attributable to the abuse, Pam stated:

Just the fact that we've both been eating all the time [laughs] and that she's kinda...we've both kinda gained weight. And I think it's just because I'm always like, "Let's eat"....But...other than that, I really don't think so. (Pam)

Gastric Distress

This was a variant somatic sequel to the abuse as reported by secondary survivor, Russ. Without prompting related to somatic effects, Russ indicated:

It [the abuse] makes me almost like sick [puts hand on stomach]....Just to think about it, too, you know. It makes me, I guess, like sick and angry both at the same time, and sad, too....[I] kinda just like, you know, like kinda just get a gut feeling. (Russ)

Although there are several possible connotations of the word "sick," here, the literal interpretation of upset stomach appears strengthened by Russ's placing of his hand on his abdomen.

Alcohol Use

Drinking alcohol to cope with discussions about the primary survivor's experience of abuse was a variant somatic response spontaneously referenced by secondary survivor, Stuart. Although somewhat vague, Stuart suggested his related use of alcohol was "probably just enough to loosen you up a little, or maybe to the depressing part of it [the abuse]. Depressed you a little bit to talk about it [the abuse]." Lisa did not refer to Stuart's use of alcohol.

SEXUAL SEQUELAE FOR PARTNERS AS SECONDARY SURVIVORS OF CHILDHOOD SEXUAL ABUSE

The sexual sequelae of childhood sexual abuse as reported by participants represented themes related to sexual behaviors, interests, and problems. In the interest of precision, this domain also encompassed themes that are specifically sexual in nature that might otherwise pertain to more general domains (i.e., feelings, thoughts, and self-perceptions about sex or sexuality). In total, 17 themes were generated by secondary survivors with regard to the sexual impact of the primary survivor's abuse on themselves. Secondary survivors reported between 2 and 11 personal sexual effects, and all did so without prompting, with the exception of Brian (Couple 1). Similarly, 22 themes were presented by primary survivors regarding sexual effects for their partners, and all primary survivors spontaneously referred to between 1 and 17 themes for their partners in the sexual domain, without prompting. In spite of the large number of themes generated in this domain, reports of sexual sequelae were diffuse and there were no themes that were universally identified for partners by all secondary and/or all primary survivors.

Accommodating Primary Survivor's Sexual Needs

Attempts to attend to and adjust for the primary survivor's sexual needs or reactions deriving from the abuse was a typical sexual sequel reported by all secondary survivors with the exception of Russ. As a specific example, Ted offered, "I try to make her feel at ease...the best I can....I always make sure there's a sheet or something...covering her." Fred also described attempts to accommodate the survivor's needs related to sexual activity, although he did admit, "Sometimes I get mad..." Angie's attempts to be accommodating were described in the context of initiating sexual activity.

Similarly all primary survivors with the exception of Russ's partner Jill reported attempts by the secondary survivor to accommodate her sexual needs. Although Kelly referred to these efforts on the part of Brian, she qualified this by stating, "I think sometimes he's too wrapped up in himself" during intercourse. In addition, Patty cited Ted's efforts to accommodate her sexual needs in the context of interrupted sexual activity, as noted with respect to that theme, below.

Sexual Dissatisfaction/Frustration

Feeling dissatisfied and frustrated with the frequency and/or nature of the sexual activity between secondary and primary survivor was a typical sequel to the abuse reported by all secondary survivors with the exception of Russ. For these secondary survivors, sexual dissatisfaction was predominantly attributed to sexual activity that was either interrupted by the primary survivor's adverse reactions or that was perceived as infrequent in frequency. Sexual dissatisfaction also occurred in the context of a variety of other themes articulated by most of these secondary survivors, including confusion regarding the source of sexual problems in the relationship, blaming one's self for sexual problems in the relationship, a decreased sense of sexual self-efficacy, and relationship conflict focused on sexual issues, thus leading to sexual frustration. Ted, in particular, characterized his sexual frustration due to the primary survivor's failure to overcome her discomfort with nudity as mild, stating, "It's not a big deal....Sometimes it's sort of frustrating, I guess because...it's just like...'Come on. It's just me'." Angie related her sexual dissatisfaction specifically to her role as serving as the active rather than receiving partner during sexual activity. Sexual dissatisfaction/frustration was also noted as a typical theme for secondary survivors by four primary survivors (Kelly, Sally, Lisa, Pam), who largely agreed with their partners' descriptions of sexual dissatisfaction.

Infrequent Sexual Activity

As noted above, infrequent sexual activity, including intercourse as well as other sexual behaviors, was cited as a typical sexual sequel to the abuse by four secondary survivors (Brian, Fred, Stuart, Angie). It is important to note that although this activity was described by these participants as infrequent ("Not having sex as often as---well, I would like"--Brian), it is not clear that the actual frequency of that activity was substantively less than that of other couples. With respect to the sexual behaviors themselves, Stuart clarified, "It's just the frequency. I mean, it's not like it was crazy when we did it, handcuffs or anything like that. I think [the frequency's] about the only...thing different about it." The perception that the frequency of sexual activity within the relationship was infrequent was shared by these secondary survivors' relationship partners (Kelly, Sally, Lisa, Pam). In a fairly typical response pattern, Kelly addressed this theme by mentioning, "I feel like...he doesn't get satisfied enough because of my not wanting to [have sex]. And we probably, maybe, have sex once a week, and that's the max."

Low Sexual Self-efficacy

A feeling among secondary survivors that they were sexually inadequate and/or undesirable was a typical sexual sequel to the abuse as reported by four primary survivors (Kelly, Sally, Lisa, Pam). This was well phrased by Sally, who noted, "If I don't have sex with him [Fred] of course he's going to--his male ego is...of course that's kicked down" and similarly, "[He'll think] something's wrong with me. I'm not doing it right." Kelly placed Brian's response of low sexual self-efficacy in the context of themes regarding confusion about the source of sexual problems in the relationship and subsequent self-blame regarding these problems. This low sense of sexual self-efficacy was also acknowledged as a variant sexual theme by three secondary survivors (Fred, Stuart, Angie). Much like the pattern Kelly reported for Brian, Fred traced his low sexual self-efficacy to his confusion and self-blame about the source of sexual problems in his relationship with Sally.

Relationship Conflict Regarding Sexual Issues

Experiencing frequent and/or intense relationship conflict in relation to sexual difficulties was presented as a typical sexual sequel to the abuse by four primary (Kelly, Sally, Lisa, Pam). In addition to the joking yet emotionally loaded conversations regarding the frequency of sexual activity reported by both Brian and Kelly, Kelly described other instances in which her physical/sexual needs were disregarded, often in the context of verbal arguments:

> Normally, he does things to annoy me [laughs]. He will normally...rub my legs just...because I know I don't want him to do that...and I'll normally shove him away and...he'll just keep doing it. Because he's bigger and stronger you can't shove him away. (Kelly)

Considerable relationship conflict about sexual concerns was also noted by three secondary (Fred, Stuart, Angie) survivors as a typical sequel to the abuse. Finally, Fred indicated that the difficulties outlined above have resulted in considerable relationship conflict specifically concerning sexual matters:

We've argued over—about sex a few times...I think the main thing—most of the time we argue about it is...like I've brought up—I've asked her about how come... she'll go through those phases [alternating sexual interest and disinterest]. And... we'll get into arguments over that...because I'll mention it and she might not want to talk about it, or I don't know, but it'll be one of them [sic] things where...she'll just get mad at me or upset. (Fred)

Stuart also highlighted considerable relationship conflict concerning sexual issues, which he attributed to the mutual sexual frustration he perceived for himself and for Lisa.

Change in Views about Sex/sexuality

A change in the secondary survivor's worldview regarding the meaning or handling of sex/sexuality was a typical sexual sequel to the abuse referenced by four primary survivors (Kelly, Sally, Patty, Jill). For two primary survivors, Patty and Jill, this theme was epitomized by the secondary survivor "not taking sex as lightly" (Patty). As phrased by Jill, "It [my abuse history] made him definitely just much more aware of--and question himself, and just the act, and what it means to him" and "just knowing that...sexuality is an extremely...fragile thing." With respect to this same theme, Kelly described a change in Brian that consisted of the development of an even more negative attitude toward pornography. In contrast, Sally was more hesitant regarding the degree of change in sexual attitudes actually achieved by Fred, stating, "But like his view on things, like he would try to be a little more considerate...but I don't think he is that considerate about it."

Changing perspectives about sex/sexuality was also a variant sexual sequel to the abuse according to two secondary survivors (Fred, Russ). For Fred, this change related specifically to his use of sexual humor: "Before I might joke about something [sexual], but...after finding out about this or whatnot...I might kind of watch what I say....kind of in general." Similarly, Russ indicated that he would be less likely to "joke" about sex or to treat the subject lightly.

Confusion Regarding Source of Sexual Problems in Relationship

Uncertainty regarding typical sexual sequel to the abuse as reported by three secondary (Fred, Stuart, Angie) As previously noted, Fred mentioned the theme of confusion regarding the source of sexual problems in the relationship as an antecedent to themes of blaming one's self for sexual problems in the relationship and decreased sexual self-efficacy. Fred did, however, indicate that this confusion diminished as a result of Sally's disclosure concerning her abuse, indicating, "Once she told me about it, it seemed like I could...I started trying to link things together....That's when I started being like, 'Oh, o.k., maybe that's why this is happening'." Confusion among secondary survivors regarding the reasons for sexual problems in the relationship was also noted by three primary survivors (Kelly, Sally, Lisa). Kelly reports, "He's said, 'Is it me?....Is it me, the reason why you don't want to have sex?', and I don't think he necessarily understands that."

Self-blame for Sexual Problems in Relationship

A tendency among secondary survivors to blame themselves for sexual problems in their relationships with the primary survivors was a typical sexual sequel to the abuse delineated by three secondary survivors (Fred, Stuart, Angie) Stuart provided more specifics with respect to his self-blame than did other secondary survivors, indicating:

> If I was alone or something, I would just start thinking of why we didn't have sex, or...what it was about me. Just kinda puttin' all the blame on myself....I was like, uh, kinda quick on the draw, so I'd think maybe that...had something to do with it....Not really experimental, maybe that had something to do with it. (Stuart)

As previously mentioned for Fred, Stuart further noted that his confusion and self-blame diminished somewhat, but not entirely, in light of Lisa's disclosure regarding her abuse:

> But then she had told me about it....Part of me didn't believe her, like saying, "No, that's not it" just to save my feelings. And...then another part of me would go, "O.K., that's [my problem is] not it" but then later on I would think about it again. (Stuart)

Similar self-blame for sexual problems was also a variant sexual sequel to the abuse discussed by two primary survivors, Sally and Kelly indicated ("I know that it makes him feel bad, because I know he probably feels like it's something he--there's something wrong with him"—Kelly).

Increased Awareness of Frequency of Sexual Activity

Heightened awareness of and sensitivity to the frequency of occurrence of sexual activity in the relationship was a typical sexual sequel to the abuse noted for secondary survivors by three primary survivors (Kelly, Sally, Pam). In this regard, Kelly provided the same example given by Brian concerning his joking that the frequency of their sexual activity "has to do with the moons." Pam related this increased awareness to the higher priority that Angie places on sexual activity as someone who was not sexually abused in childhood. This focus on the frequency of sexual activity was also a variant sexual sequel that Brian described for himself as a secondary survivor: "I took a calendar one time [laughs] and made a bunch of "X's" or whatever on the different days....I did it on...the last two times that I knew we had made love."

Blocking Thoughts of Primary Survivor's Abuse during Sexual Activity

Making an effort to block out or ignore thoughts about the primary survivor's abuse that may arise during sexual activity was a variant sexual sequel to the abuse cited by two secondary survivors (Brian, Fred). As Brian said, "I don't want to go there, you know? There's no sense in me getting all worked up about it." The secondary survivor's attempts to block thoughts of the abuse during sexual activity were also reported as a variant sequel to the abuse by Brian and Fred's respective relationship partners (Kelly, Sally). Although Kelly did not think Brian experienced thoughts of her sexual abuse during intercourse, she did not recognize this as the more active or purposeful process of blocking thoughts alluded to by Brian: "I don't think he is probably even thinking at that point [when physically intimate] about that. I don't think that that [the abuse] probably even enters in his mind at that point" (Kelly).

Higher Priority on Sexual Activity

The perception that the secondary survivor placed a higher priority and value on sexual activity than did the primary survivor was a typical sexual sequel to the abuse presented by three primary survivors (Sally, Lisa, Pam). The vicarious influence of the abuse for the secondary survivor is illustrated in this theme when the primary survivor experiences a diminished interest in sex as a direct result of the abuse, leaving the secondary survivor with the appearance of having an abnormally high libido ("He [Fred] wants it all the time"--Sally) or the appearance of unduly emphasizing the sexual aspect of the relationship. As one example, Pam emphasized the characterological aspect of Angie's perceived tendency to place a higher priority on sexual activity: "I think a lot of her life is based on...sex. Like she's a very sexual person, and I think...it's very important to her. Very, very important to her." This theme is also implied by the reports of those participants who indicated sexual frustration and/or increased awareness of frequency of sexual activity among secondary survivors, above.

Few Sexual Sequelae

In a variant theme, two secondary survivors (Ted, Russ) indicated that the primary survivor's abuse had very limited effect on their sexual relationship. For both of these men, the relative lack of adverse effect in the sexual domain as compared with other secondary survivors appeared to be linked to their perceptions that the experience of childhood sexual abuse was without many sexual repercussions for the primary survivor. For example, Ted indicated that sexual sequelae for Patty were limited to her discomfort with nudity: "Otherwise, it's...pretty normal. I think it's pretty good, really," and analysis of Ted's other statements concerning sexual issues yielded only two mild sexual themes for him related to Patty's abuse. In a variant response among primary survivors, Jill concurred with Russ's belief that sexual effects on him had been negligible, in general.

Interrupted Sexual Activity

Interruptions during sexual activity due to the primary survivor's adverse reactions related to her abuse was referenced as a variant sexual sequel to the abuse as presented by two primary survivors (Sally, Patty) and by one secondary survivor (Fred). By both Sally and Fred, this theme was implicated as a key contributor to the theme of sexual dissatisfaction/frustration, coupled with infrequent sexual activity, as described above. Patty made specific note of Ted's supportiveness and ability to accommodate such interruptions well.

Use of Countering Behaviors to Promote Sexual Activity

The secondary survivor's use of instrumental strategies in an attempt to combat and undo adverse effects of the abuse and thereby facilitate sexual activity with the primary survivor was described as a variant sexual sequel to the abuse by two primary survivors (Kelly, Lisa) and by one secondary survivor (Brian). Such countering behaviors were best articulated by Brian, who reported employing them for their positive non-sexual as well as sexual effect on the primary survivor:

> I've did [sic] stuff like that. I've bought her flowers on bad days that I knew was gonna be bad. And on days that's gonna be bad--this is a good one, I do it a lot-- I write her little notes and put in the house...I'll put notes on her car....I used to... buy her...different stuff. Anyways, I used to do stuff like that on bad days, and that made a big difference [in her attitude]....It made a little difference there*[sexually] too. (Brian)*

Kelly also addressed this use of countering behaviors by Brian to attempt to ease sexual tensions and promote sexual activity, but she did not refer to the broader range of countering behaviors (i.e., gifts, notes) that Brian described apart from those used instrumentally to promote sexual activity.

Lisa's reference to the use of countering behaviors by Stuart focused on his attempts to use sexual humor to get her to "lighten up," but resulted in a negative response by Lisa:

> I think...what he's adapted was this: "I'll make a joke out of it and then it will be o.k." But I got really irritated because he was really fixated on sex...that's what really bothered me. And I think that's because...I wouldn't have sex with him. He started, just if he saw something on T.V...some dirty stupid thing. He would just be really explicit. (Lisa)

Infrequent Nonsexual Touch

A diminished frequency of nonsexual forms of touch between partners was a variant sexual sequel to the abuse as reported by two primary survivors (Lisa, Pam) and by one secondary survivor (Angie). As Lisa related, "I could not conceive that he [Stuart] would want to touch me if it wasn't sexual so, as a consequence, I've avoided touching him." Pam also reported, "...it was bad because everybody, all of our friends were teasing us, and they're all, you know, because we're—we're not a very physically close couple. Like we wouldn't sit next to each other and we wouldn't, uh, talk about sex all the time, and so our friends always tease us."

Infrequent Sexual Discussion

As a continuation of the previous theme, a paucity of conversation about the sexual relationship with the primary survivor and sexual topics in general constituted a variant sexual sequel to the abuse for secondary survivors as reported by two primary survivors (Lisa, Pam) and by one secondary survivor (Angie). In this respect, Pam related, "Mmm, well, I—you know—I kind of avoid the subject a lot. And I don't think—Angie doesn't approach me with it about—a lot in conversations..."

Pervasive/profound Sexual Sequelae

In contrast to those who reported few adverse sexual effects, two secondary survivors (Brian, Stuart) endorsed a variant theme of pervasive and/or profound sexual sequelae to the abuse. as presented by two secondary survivors (Brian, Stuart). In the most interesting related response, Brian initially did not refer to any sexual sequelae for him related to Kelly's history of abuse, and denied such effects when queried. However, he appeared to change his mind regarding the disclosure of this information within a few moments and revoked his denial, declaring emphatically, "I take that back. Yes, I do [heavy emphasis]. It has affected me a lot [emphasis] sexually." Brian then went on to describe seven themes pertaining to the sexual domain. Although discussing a broader range of sequelae during other portions of his interview, Stuart on one occasion indicated that the sexual realm constituted the sole area of his relationship with Lisa that had been affected by her sexual abuse, noting seven sexual themes. In light of this emphasis, the sexual domain would appear to be a very salient domain of impact for Stuart.

Accusatory Stance toward Primary Survivor's Sexuality

As a particular variant of relationship conflict, two primary survivors (Sally, Lisa). noted that the secondary survivor adopted an accusatory and judgmental stance regarding the primary survivor's sexuality or sexual history (calling Lisa a "slut") as an abuse-related theme. According to Sally, "Sometimes he [Fred] does blame himself but...he, in general, he's always giving me a hard time").

Second-guessing Primary Survivor's Sexual Self-knowledge

The secondary survivor's seeming refusal to accept the primary survivor's description of her sexual needs and reactions at face value, and his consistent questioning of her self-knowledge related to sex, was articulated as a variant sexual sequel to the abuse as presented by one secondary (Brian) and one primary (Sally) survivor. This is illustrated by the intensity of Kelly's description of her dislike of sexual intercourse ("I do not like sex. I just don't like it....As far as the...intercourse goes, I don't. I don't like that at all....I just dread it") and yet Brian's apparent discounting and equivocating of this:

> She says that—she'll say, 'I hate sex'....I know that she doesn't really. I mean, I know what she's talking about....You just have to get past that certain point [sexually]...That's what I'm telling you. I think it's just a lot of the thought [emphasis] initially. (Brian)

From the primary survivor's perspective, Sally described Fred as negating her own feelings of low sexual self-efficacy.

Assuming Role of More Active Partner during Sexual Activity

The tendency of the secondary survivor to adopt the role of the more active partner during sexual encounters was a variant sequel to the abuse reported by Couple Six, Angie and Pam. Angie indicated, "Well...you know, [sex is] like a give and take kind of thing, and I don't...receive like as much as I give," and estimated that she is the more active in terms of providing pleasure to her partner "probably eighty percent of the time." A related theme of sexual dissatisfaction/frustration was noted for Angie by both partners.

Difficulty Initiating Sexual Activity

Having trouble determining when to initiate sexual activity, and when not to, and therefore hesitating in this regard was a variant sexual sequel to the abuse provided by one secondary survivor (Angie). Specifically, Angie remarked:

It's just hard to gauge. Like sometimes [pause], sometimes I don't know, like [if] she says she wants to make love, if it's because she thinks I want to, or if it's because…It's really, like it's tricky. (Angie)

Sexualizing

A tendency by the secondary survivor to inappropriately sexualize all aspects of the relationship with the primary survivor was noted as a variant sexual sequel by one primary survivor (Sally). Specifically, Sally described Fred as sexualizing all expressions of affection ("It's always a sexual thing. If…he's got his hands on me, it's got to be here [touches inner thigh] instead of…just put your arm around my shoulder. Or you've got to be kissing lips instead of kissing cheeks"). As viewed by Sally, companion themes for Fred were those of placing a higher priority on sexual activity than the primary survivor and of sexual dissatisfaction/frustration.

Issuing Sexual Ultimatums

Threats by the secondary survivor to leave the relationship if the primary survivor suspending sexual activity to work on personal or relationship problems related to the abuse was a variant sexual sequel stated by one primary survivor (Sally), and one that draws attention to the potential for re-victimization within the secondary-primary survivor relationship. Specifically, Sally reported:

> …about a half a year or so ago, there was a point in time we were arguing, and I said, "Well, you know, we're arguing all the time, we can't get along, the way I see it, we either break up or we can try to work on things but no sex. Just no." But…it all happened; it didn't happen. Initially, it was, "No, we've dated for almost a year now, and I don't think that's right for you to— [this is him]—for you to ask me for that. Um, I can't do that." So pretty much, "I'm not going to date you unless you have sex with me," and I've never felt so shitty in my life; it still somehow got turned around, "Oh, it wasn't that bad," and we ended up having sex anyways. (Sally)

Apologetic Regarding Own Sexuality

One primary survivor (Sally) related a variant sexual sequel to the abuse that consisted of the secondary survivor being apologetic regarding his own sexuality and sexual needs ("I'm sorry. Maybe I'm too horny"--Fred). Sally was unclear about the extent to which she viewed this as the result of a true guilt response by Fred as opposed to a manipulative ploy.

Overemphasis on Sexual Effects of the Abuse

The tendency of the secondary survivor to place to give too much attention to the sexual repercussions of the abuse at the expense of all other sequelae was a variant sexual sequel related by one primary survivor (Pam). As phrased by Pam:

> I think it would surprise her to know how much it really affects me, you know what I mean, like the way it would. Like I thinks he just thinks it's more sexual than anything. (Pam)

And:

> Like I think she thinks it [the abuse] just all has to do with sex...and it doesn't have anything else to do with my everyday life...And I don't think she realizes how much *it affects me...in our closeness. Which is kinda easy to get. (Pam)*

ACADEMIC/CAREER SEQUELAE FOR PARTNERS AS SECONDARY SURVIVORS OF CHILDHOOD SEXUAL ABUSE

The academic and career-related sequelae of childhood sexual abuse that emerged from participant interviews consisted of themes related to various aspects of school and work. These themes were presented as they interplay with other abuse-related effects, where evident. In general, two of six secondary survivors and two of six primary survivors referred spontaneously to some academic- or career-related impact of abuse for secondary survivors, without prompting. Two additional secondary survivors reported such sequelae when prompted. The number of themes presented by individual secondary survivors ranged from zero to two, with a total of three themes. Similarly, each primary survivor offered a range of zero to two themes regarding effects on their partners, for a total of three discrete themes. There were no academic- or career-related sequelae for secondary survivors that were universally noted by all primary and/or secondary survivors, as consistent with the relative paucity of total themes presented in this domain.

Few Academic/Career Sequelae

As noted above, a typical response by secondary survivors (Brian, Ted, Russ) was to indicate that their studies and work were generally unaffected by that the primary survivor's abuse history. Although Brian indicated, when queried, that Kelly's history of sexual abuse has had no effect on his own career-related experiences, he did go on to indicate a chain of events in which relationship conflict ultimately results from Kelly's academic/career issues which they both perceive to stem from her abuse. When prompted, Russ initially indicated that there was no effect on his academic life related to Jill's abuse. He then returned to this question and adjusted his response to indicate one such effect, that of decreased study time. Three primary survivors (Sally, Lisa, Patty) also reported that there were no academic or career-related effects of the abuse for their partners.

Decreased Study Time

Less time for secondary survivors to devote to personal studies and intellectual interests as a result of the primary survivor's abuse was a typical academic/career sequel to the abuse as perceived by three secondary survivors (Fred, Russ, Angie). Academically, Fred spontaneously stated that Sally's abuse affected him by virtue of decreased time and productivity. In this regard, he stated, "Because she requires so much attention and...things like that...I have a hard having time to do all the things I need to do and then see her as much as she wants me to be around her." Russ similarly reported interference in his studies as a result of caring for Jill during a time period when she was experiencing problems, although he was unsure to what extent those problems related to her abuse:

> Can I go back to that one [laughs]?....There was a period of time where she would call me all the time to come get her....I don't know if that was--I don't think that was really...her not trusting me being down there [away at

school] myself. So I don't know if that really had an effect....unless it was like insecurity things or things that she was dealing with at the time. (Russ)

Finally, Angie indicated that she experienced decreased study time in relation to Pam's history of abuse, stating, "I feel like I have to take care of her....I feel like I should spend time with her, and so that takes away from my study time."

Decreased study time for secondary survivors was also reported by two primary survivors (Jill, Pam). When queried, Jill clearly placed Russ's struggles to manage school and caretaking in the context of a bout of self-described depression related to her abuse:

> There was a time period, about three years ago, when I was so depressed...I just couldn't get out of bed....He was living in [another town], and...he would drive me back up to [own town]...at like 5 o'clock in the morning, and then drive back down, and go to class all day, come back and get me....It was ridiculous....That's something that I feel very bad about, but...I was in such a stupor at the time. So that definitely affected his studies, then, because he...was trying really hard. He had some really hard classes, and that prevented him from giving...a lot of his attention to that. (Jill)

A similar theme was also noted by Pam, although she attributed Angie's loss of study time to Angie's own neediness in addition to the abuse:

> She's got finals next week, and...she won't study for them when I'm around.... When she studies, I have to leave. I have to leave the house, because she can't do it with me around, because all she wants to do is be right there with me....I don't need Angie by my side at all times, but....she always needs me right there, unless I tell her. (Pam)

Use of Studies/work as a Distraction

The theme of focusing on school and/or work to distract from abuse-related difficulties was a variant academic/career sequel reported by secondary survivor, Stuart, who spontaneously expressed a tendency to use his studies as a means of avoiding thoughts concerning Lisa's abuse. Specifically, Stuart indicated: "I just wanted to stop thinking about it, so I'd start thinking about something else. Something easier to think about....Just switch gears. Start thinking about homework or something." In contrast, Lisa reported that there was no effect on Stuart's academics as a result of her abuse.

Decreased Productivity

This theme, a variant academic/career sequel to the abuse, was cited by secondary survivor Fred as an extension of the theme of decreased study time. In this regard, Fred stated, "Because she requires so much attention and...things like that...I have a hard time having time to do all the things I need to do and then see her as much as she wants me to be around her."

Intrusive Thoughts of Primary Survivor's Childhood Sexual Abuse at Work

The theme of experiencing unwanted thoughts of the primary survivor's abuse history while working was a variant academic/career sequel to the abuse noted by primary survivor, Kelly. Specifically, she reported that Brian experiences thoughts related to her sexual abuse while on the job:

> I know that he's said to me...in the past that...whenever he's at work, you know, just nailing up a wall or whatever, he'll say..."I was thinking about that [the abuse] today." And it makes him really mad. I can tell it makes him really mad. (Kelly)

SOCIAL SEQUELAE FOR PARTNERS AS SECONDARY SURVIVORS OF CHILDHOOD SEXUAL ABUSE

The social sequelae of childhood sexual abuse for primary and secondary survivors, as expressed by participants, centered on the frequency and nature of social interactions and interpersonal relationships between the secondary and primary survivor as well as between the secondary survivor and others. In the interest of specificity, information that might otherwise be included in another domain was subsumed under the social domain if it pertained primarily to a social phenomenon (e.g., thoughts or feelings regarding social events or interactions). Relationship conflict was included herein if it did not clearly pertain to another domain (e.g., relationship conflict concerning sexual or career issues were included in those domains).

A total of 11 social sequelae of childhood sexual abuse were presented by secondary survivors concerning their own experience in regard to their partners' abuse. The number of such themes generated by each secondary survivor ranged from three to eight. In a similar pattern, a total of 11 themes regarding the secondary effects of childhood sexual abuse on the social experience of their partners were articulated by primary survivors, with individual primary survivors reporting between zero and eight themes. All participants (both primary and secondary survivors), with the exception of Ted (Couple 4), offered responses in the social domain without benefit of prompting. There were no social sequelae for secondary survivors that were attributed to the primary survivor's childhood sexual abuse by all secondary and/or all primary survivors.

Increased Empathy for Others

Experiencing a greater capacity for empathy toward others was a typical social sequel to the abuse as reported by four secondary survivors (Brian, Fred, Stuart, Russ). For instance, Brian reported enhanced empathy for others, including other victims and children, which may represent a kind of generalization of his empathy for Kelly to other persons and situations. He also specifically extended this theme to include other secondary survivors:

> I understand completely why you get some people that...I mean, I would never think of doing this, but I can understand...like people that kill one another and stuff over similar situations....I can completely [emphasis] put that together and understand why people do stuff they do. (Brian)

Similarly, Stuart indicated, "I guess I may be just more sympathetic towards it, but I don't think it really affected it much....I think I've gained a bit of understanding."

The theme of increased empathy was also reported by these secondary survivors' relationship partners (Kelly, Sally, Lisa, Jill). Regarding the increase in Brian's empathy, Kelly reported:

> I would think that probably because he knows how much it's affected me, he probably has a better, or a greater, capacity for empathy for other people who've experienced similar things....I'm sure he would be more...compassionate to talk to about something like that than somebody who doesn't really have anything that's close to them. (Kelly)

Both Sally and Lisa noted enhanced empathy for their partners, but to a lesser degree of certainty. As stated by Sally, "Like...with the feeling...I think he's maybe realizing more...how it [abuse] affects women, and puttin' more credit to where it's due, but [pauses] I don't know if it really has changed his beliefs or not" and by Lisa, "I don't think it's kicked in, but I think that eventually he'll probably see that he can be a very understanding person. I don't think that he is at a point in his life where he's ready to realize anything good about himself right now."

Relationship Conflict with Primary Survivor

Conflict in the secondary-primary survivor relationship that was attributed to the abuse was a typical social sequel to the abuse as reported by all primary survivors with the exception of Patty. For all of these primary survivors, the relationship conflict appeared to emanate from a combination of both the sexual abuse and the nature of the secondary survivor's personality and coping style. As alluded to by Kelly:

'Cause sometimes I get upset and I don't even know why I'm mad, and why did his saying just something really miniscule even set me off?....And then whenever I get mad, I just need that little bit of space or time away from him to figure out why I'm mad. And he won't let me do that. He...will not let me have a little bit of time to...not talk....He will be right there with me. (Kelly)

The relationship conflict reported by Sally was attributed not only to her abuse but also to Fred's perceived difficulties with emotional intimacy. A similar pattern was exhibited by Pam, who noted relationship conflict but tentatively attributed this to a possible combination of Angie's own "neediness" as well as abuse-oriented issues:

I think that maybe it's just the kind of person that she is. I don't know. I'm not really sure. I mean, it could be--like this is kind of a long shot--I mean you could connect it to the point like maybe sexually she's not as close to me, so she tries to make up for it in other ways, but I'm not really sure. (Pam)

The theme of relationship conflict between secondary and primary survivor was also articulated by three secondary survivors (Fred, Russ, Angie). According to Fred, "It seems like every time that kind of thing [social] would come up, that would be one of the nights where we would get into a big argument." Russ also described relationship conflict, resulting in loss of intimacy, focused on Jill's possessiveness of him and his beliefs regarding her infidelity attributed to the abuse:

> It's in...like the little things, like if I want to go out with my friends...a lot more than she thinks I should....That would get her mad, and that would in turn get me angry with her, and...sometimes it's made it to where I didn't want to be around her as much. (Russ)

Finally, Angie also indicated relationship conflict related to Pam's socializing with others in addition to their sexual issues and Pam's substance-abuse issues:

> She'll [Pam will] get upset that she feels like she's always going out without me. Like...we recently had a big fight about this. She feels like she always goes out without me, and that she should stay in because she thinks I'll be upset because she's going out. And...sometimes I'll care, like if I've studied all day and I've saved two hours to do something with her and she's doing something else...then I'll be upset. (Angie)

Loss of Social Contacts

Difficulty maintaining strong social ties outside of the relationship with the primary survivor due to reluctance to leave the primary survivor to cope with her issues alone was also a typical social theme reported by all secondary survivors with the exception of Stuart. This difficulty involved in remaining connected to others was referenced by Brian:

> I'm supposed to go to Big Bear for two weeks on a Outdoor Club deer hunt, clear up in a high elevation....No phone or nothing...and I've been trying to think up a program that I can put together for that episode. I'm just showing you ways I defend against it, I guess. (Brian)

Fred also noted compromising the frequency and/or intensity of his social connections due to Sally's abuse-related struggles, at times leading to relationship conflict:

> There was a phase where she wouldn't--she felt like she didn't want to go out [to social events] with me...She didn't want to go out like to friends' houses or out to a bar with me....Usually I would end up staying [with Sally] and not going (Fred)

And:

I've...not like lost friendships, but I've lost...how close I was to a lot of my friends before I started going out with her, because she requires so much attention....My friendship level of my friends have [sic] gone...down, because I just don't...hang out with the people that I used to anymore because I just never have time. (Fred)

And for Ted:

Because we spend a lot of time together...it's hard to see other people. And I really don't know what to do about that. Because I don't want her to think that I'm...ditching her or blowing her off, or not interested, or don't want to see her. (Ted)

Angie also related her loss of social contacts to a reluctance to leave Pam alone, as did the other secondary survivors. However, she went on to uniquely link her social isolation specifically to a decrease in self-confidence and self-efficacy resulting from her perceived unsuccessful attempts to interact with Pam, which generalized to other people:

I'm not nearly [emphasis] as much of a huggy person as I used to be, and it trans--it like goes to all my relationships now....I'm very much muted in all my interactions with other people. (Angie)

And similarly:

It used to be really easy for me to make friends, because...I didn't feel at all self-conscious....and like now, 'cause I doubt myself about this all the time, I don't feel as confident like even when I'm interacting with people that I don't know very well, and so like I'm just quiet. (Angie)

The secondary survivor's loss of social connections outside the relationship was a variant social sequel to the abuse acknowledged by one primary survivor, Jill. Although Patty noted Ted's reluctance to leave her alone, stating, "Like last night he...went up for class...and he was staying longer, so he didn't get back yet. But he was like..."Are you going to be O.K.?", and he always...he knows," she did not voice awareness of the larger social ramifications of this for Ted. In fact, Patty indicated, "We have been together a lot, but...I think he has pretty good...healthy relationships with his friends and stuff...and that all that still seems pretty healthy." Lastly, Pam noted Angie's loss of social contacts, but did not view this as an abuse-related theme. Rather, Pam presented this as related solely to Angie's studying and did not refer to any of the decrements in social self-efficacy mentioned by Angie.

Loss of Intimacy with Primary Survivor

A decrease in the perceived amount of closeness and connection between the secondary and primary survivor was cited as a typical social sequel to the abuse by three secondary survivors (Ted, Russ, Angie). As articulated by Angie, "Like I keep thinking...there's some barrier between our intimacy. Like she'll [Pam will] get upset that I'll get upset because...we can't connect, or we can't talk." Ted attributed this loss of intimacy to the fact that both he and Patty bottle up their feelings rather than discussing her abuse. Finally, Russ cited loss of intimacy with the primary survivor resulting from relationship conflict due to or exacerbated by the abuse. This loss of intimacy was also recognized as a variant theme by two primary survivors (Jill, Pam). As Jill noted, "Over the past year he withdrew a lot, and got less and less...he's became [sic] less and less emotionally involved. I think he made himself do that."

Difficult Relationships with Primary Survivor's Family of Origin

Difficulty relating to the primary survivor's family who perpetrated or allowed the abuse was observed to be a typical social sequel to the abuse according to three secondary survivors (Brian, Fred, Angie). As Brian described the difficulty navigating these relationships:

> One time, we got on the subject over at her parent's house. That was a big mistake....Her mother and dad, of course you're aware that she told them about it but they didn't believe her....We got on the subject of [the perpetrator], then it led to this. So it wasn't good. (Brian)

Difficulty relating to the primary survivor's family of origin was likewise reported by the relationship partners of two of these secondary survivors (Kelly, Pam).

Change in View of Others

A change in worldview related to how one sees others, in general, and to trust, in particular, was a typical social sequel to the abuse for secondary survivors as viewed by three primary survivors (Kelly, Lisa, Jill). To illustrate, Kelly surmised that Brian is more judgmental of others as a consequence of knowing about her abuse, stating, "I would tend to think that he would probably be more judgmental to people who are taking advantage of other people." Lisa proposed an even more general change in her partner's view of others so as to be more accurate or realistic, stating, "I think that maybe he [Stuart]...has kinda lost some of his illusions about people." Beyond mere disillusionment, Lisa also expressed fears that her partner's awareness of her abuse may have contributed to his tendency to instrumentally use negative information to gain the upper hand in their relationship:

> I think that my abuse became kind of like his little chip, like that's...his poker chip, that he knows that despite being really strong and really out there and really pushy, that I had this huge, huge secret, and I think that that [becomes tearful]...like he realized that I had a huge weakness, that...I had huge parts of myself that I didn't like....And he can put up with the fact that I've orchestrated everything, because he can say, "Well, she may think she's pretty hot. She may think she's got it all together, but she's got this dirty little secret." (Lisa)

A change in one's perceptions about human nature was likewise a variant sequel to the abuse as reported by two secondary survivors (Ted, Russ) Specifically, Ted reported, "I sort of share her [Patty's] belief that...humans are generally--they're not that great [laughs]....They're selfish or whatever...and this [her abuse] may reinforce it a bit." For Russ, this was characterized by an increased tendency to distrust.

Stagnant Relationship with Primary Survivor

The perception that the secondary-primary survivor relationship was stunted and not growing or moving forward in a healthy way was a typical social sequel to the abuse reported by three primary survivors (Sally, Lisa, Jill). This stagnant feel to the relationship was captured by Jill: "He...felt the relationship was going nowhere, and I would pull so many manipulative tricks....I don't know if he even knows why he's stuck around for so many years." For Sally, the "stuck" properties of her relationship with Stuart was attributed to a combination of her abuse and of Fred's perceived difficulties with emotional intimacy in general.

This kind of stagnating relationship was also a variant theme reported by Russ as a secondary survivor in the context of relationship conflict and loss of intimacy:

> There was a period when I thought that...her whole non-trust thing was maybe just because she was doing something [sexual] herself....Then, after a while, I just got to a point where, and this is bad, especially when you're in a relationship, but I think I just got to a point where I just didn't care so much anymore....I think a lot of that was...just my way of dealing with going out, breaking up, and going out, and breaking up [laughs]. I just thought, "Well, I'm not going to put everything into it anymore...I'll give her a little bit here and there, but that's it." (Russ)

This phenomenon formed a constellation of themes leading to a questioning of the long-term viability of the relationship and, ultimately, a change in the permanency status of the relationship for several of these couples.

Questioning Long-term Viability of Intimate Relationship

Questioning the long-term viability of intimate relationships, either with the secondary survivor or with others, as a consequence of the abuse was a variant social sequel to the abuse indicated by two secondary survivors (Ted, Russ). For Ted:

> [Talking about abuse sequelae for Patty and for him] That's just going into depths that I don't think that we'll ever go to [laughs]....We just haven't really talked about our feelings in that great of detail...and I just don't see it happening anytime soon....For now it's O.K....Maybe not forever...but I...don't know if it would be like that forever. (Ted)

Similarly, Russ questioned, "I really don't know that her and I are meant to be together right now."

This fragility was also a variant social sequel reported by two primary survivors, including Jill who acknowledged, "Even just recently, like over the summer, Russ wanted to leave me, and he wasn't happy..." Lisa also generalized this questioning of relationships by Stuart beyond the context of their current relationship, surmising, "I think he'd probably not have another relationship for a long time."

Change in Status of Relationship with Primary Survivor

As a result of stagnation in the secondary-primary survivor relationship, two couples (Stuart and Lisa, Russ and Jill) reported a variant social theme of downgrading their level of commitment to the relationship and changing the relationship's course from a long term commitment to marriage or dating to the decision to the decision to separate at present (Russ and Jill) or upon college graduation (Stuart and Lisa). Stuart, for example, indicated that Lisa's experience of childhood sexual abuse, and the sexual discord it has caused in their relationship, is the sole contributor to the fact that they no longer intend to stay together as a couple beyond graduation:

> We had originally planned just to get married and stuff like that on down the road, but...now....Maybe just a little bit upset just because the entire, the whole relationship is good except for one thing [sex]. It's just kind of annoying to have one...bad thing in the relationship. And I figured that we would work through it or get over it. (Stuart)

As with Stuart, Russ also articulated the pattern of themes connecting relationship conflict with a questioning of the viability of the relationship, and, ultimately, an altered course for the relationship, in this instance the decision to take a "cooling period" in their relationship and to re-evaluate their plans for a long-term partnership. Lisa concurred about altered status of relationship, for different reasons (control issues and sexual concerns related to her abuse. In contrast, other secondary (Brian, Ted) and primary (Patty) survivors indicated that they maintain a good relationship in spite of difficulties associated with the abuse.

Social Stigma

Feeling awkward about the abuse in social situations was cited as a variant social sequel to the abuse by two secondary survivors (Stuart, Ted). Awkwardness. This sense of social embarrassment or constraint was captured by Stuart, who stated, "When I talk about it I'm a little embarrassed, I think, maybe. Just talking about it. Uh, maybe it's just social taboos. I think that--It's not something you talk about over dinner [laughs] at a restaurant." Also in regard to his peers, Ted indicated some small degree of social embarrassment or constraint related to Patty's childhood sexual abuse, but specifically when accounting for her social distancing to others: "They [friends] sometimes ask me why they never see her...And...I can't really say exactly why. You know, I don't--I'm not going to tell them, 'She doesn't want to meet people because of this [the abuse]'." Neither of the primary survivors referenced here voiced awareness of this theme for the secondary survivor.

Social Ridicule

In a related theme, Brian described a variant social sequel to the abuse involving subjecting himself to social ridicule as a result of his attentiveness to the survivor. Although he has not been teased specifically about Kelly's abuse, of which others are unaware, he feels the teasing may be indirectly related to the extent that the abuse effects his interactions with Kelly, particularly his reluctance to leave her alone. For example, Brian indicated of his male friends and coworkers, "Everybody thinks I'm like a big marshmallow...and it doesn't bother me at all, really."

Avoidance of Primary Survivor's Family of Origin

Beyond the theme of difficult interactions with the primary survivor's family of origin, a clear avoidance of family interactions by the secondary survivor was cited as a variant social sequel to the abuse by Sally:

> He [Fred] don't [sic] like to visit there a lot....He didn't want to walk down to meet my parents. He wouldn't come in because he didn't want to get his dog muddy. He wanted to hurry up and get to his mom's. Anyhow, I personally thought that they were both lame excuses....To throw in the dog thing, what was that [laughs]?! (Sally)

Loss of Normal Relationship with Primary Survivor

A theme of secondary survivor loss, here specifically related to the loss of a normal relationship uncomplicated by abuse issues, was referenced as a variant social sequel to the abuse by Pam as a primary survivor. As Pam observed, "She's [Pam has] lost normality in a relationship, I think. This isn't a typical relationship, I don't think....Like it's not like probably as fun as it would be, because it's probably just as much work for her." This was the sole social theme presented by Pam that was not articulated by Angie.

DISCUSSION

This qualitative study represents the most in-depth and complex exploration of the sequelae of abuse for the partners of female childhood sexual abuse survivors. Results delineate 96 total themes describing the experiences of these individuals as perceived by both secondary and primary survivors. These themes comprised six basic domains, including sexual sequelae (n = 25), self-perceptual sequelae (n = 18), cognitive sequelae (n = 17), affective sequelae (n = 14), social sequelae (n = 13), academic/career sequelae (n = 5), and somatic sequelae (n = 4).

Collectively, results substantiate and extend previous literature regarding the nature of childhood sexual abuse sequelae for secondary survivors. In particular, two important patterns emerged that generate worthy theoretical tenets and hypotheses for further study. First, the sequelae presented here are more diffuse than would be suggested by the secondary traumatic stress model popularized by Figley (1986; 1988a; 1995), as Finkelhor (1987) had previously theorized. Second, the secondary sequelae that emerged in the present study do not appear to contradict those suggested by previous descriptive studies, but appear to be more numerous and comprehensive in nature, including some positive experiences in the wake of the abuse that merit research and clinical attention.

With respect to the diffuse nature of the secondary trauma, many of the sequelae of childhood sexual abuse reported by and for secondary survivors were not the same as those presented by and for primary survivors (for themes relevant to primary survivors, see Wiersma, 1999). Thus, for the present sample, childhood sexual abuse did not appear to represent a "shared experience" for primary and secondary survivors in that sense. In particular, participating secondary survivors did not report many of the symptoms (e.g., dissociative phenomena, nightmares, etc.) that would suggest a full-blown traumatic stress disorder. Clearly, for these secondary survivors, the childhood sexual abuse of a partner did not result in marked physical responses (depersonalization, muscle tension, increased or decreased libido, irritability, increased alcohol intake, tearfulness, anxiety, ideas of reference, insomnia, worry, headaches, restlessness, destructiveness, hypochondria, and loss of interest in normal activities) as has been previously suggested for male partners of women raped in adulthood (Bateman and Mendelson, 1989; Rodkin et al, 1982) as well as other populations. Somatic sequelae, in fact, constituted the least cited domain of response for participating secondary survivors.

These findings reinforce the notion that the sequelae of childhood sexual abuse for secondary survivors are complex phenomena that extend beyond Figley's (1995) conceptualization of Secondary Traumatic Stress Disorder (STSD) as a clinical syndrome to include a broader range of abuse-related responses. The sequelae experienced by secondary survivors of childhood sexual abuse will not necessarily include the diagnostic criteria associated with STSD, and may be likely to involve a vast array of experiences not included in such criteria. In this way, the sequelae of the abuse described for secondary survivors were reminiscent of the vicarious effects described for helping professionals who treat primary survivors of sexual abuse (McCann and Pearlman, 1990; Pearlman and Saakvitne, 1995).

In further support of this notion, some secondary survivors presented themes reflective of adjustment and coping in the wake of the abuse, rather than negative symptomotology. Although such responses could not be considered to be direct effects of the childhood sexual abuse per se or to be part of a psychological syndrome or disorder, they may nonetheless transpire in the wake of childhood sexual abuse and therefore represent important dimensions for research and for assessment and treatment in clinical settings.

Furthermore, consideration of the positive responses offered by secondary survivors is particularly important given its relevance to the current emphasis within the field on the positive psychology movement (Myers, 1992; Snyder and Lopez, 2002). It would appear that the positive emotions, the desirable self-perceptual changes, and beneficial cognitive shifts asserted by some secondary survivors and attributed to them by some of their primary survivor partners constitute crucial resources that can be used to assist in the recovery process for both members of such couples. There may be particular promise in attending to the positive affect that was recounted by some secondary survivors but that went entirely unacknowledged by primary survivors in their descriptions of the secondary survivors' responses to the abuse, and drawing on such strength at appropriate junctures in treatment.

In addition, these reports of secondary posttraumatic growth are suggestive of important resiliency characteristics among secondary survivors that are worthy of further study. The concept of posttraumatic growth is sometimes noted for primary survivors of a variety of traumatic events (Tedeschi, Park, and Calhoun, 1998), albeit less often than a more pathology-oriented approach, and often as an apparent afterthought. There is even less available research regarding *secondary* posttraumatic growth in general, or for secondary survivors in particular Bacon and Lein, 1996; Brittain and Merriam, 1988; Burgoff, 1993; Cohen, 1988; Ferguson, 1991), and important constructs from the positive psychology movement have not been widely applied to this population.

With regard to these resiliency characteristics, there have been a number of variables cited that may serve to moderate effects of the abuse for primary survivors, but it remains unclear what these factors affecting prognosis may be for secondary survivors. For example, despite strong empirical evidence that childhood sexual abuse may be associated with a wide range of detrimental long-term sequelae, it does not appear that serious psychosocial impairment among adult female survivors is inevitable. Based on their review of empirical studies of clinical and nonclinical populations, Browne and Finkelhor (1986) concluded that survivors of childhood sexual abuse might manifest problems in psychological functioning nearly double that of their nonvictimized counterparts. However, only about one-fifth of survivors of a range of sexually abusive experiences in childhood demonstrate serious psychopathology in adulthood. Others may experience no notable negative long-term effects, or more subtle, diffuse, isolated symptoms that do not constitute a full-blown psychological disorder.

Similarly, as pointed out by Jehu, Klassen, and Gazan (1985), there may in fact be three populations of childhood sexual abuse survivors, including (a) the total population of adult females abused as children, (b) a subgroup of that population who experience psychological difficulties, and (c) a further division of this subgroup who seek help for those difficulties in clinical settings. As of yet, the relative sizes of these groups and the factors that determine membership in each have not been fully and conclusively determined (Jehu et al., 1985). Similarly, a number of studies reviewed by Kilpatrick (1987) document a significant percentage of childhood sexual abuse survivors who show few permanently harmful effects as adults, leading Kilpatrick to conclude that the relationship between childhood sexual abuse and adult maladjustment is not necessarily a linear causal one. Similarly, it may be that a portion of secondary survivors of childhood sexual abuse may meet the diagnostic criteria for STSD, and others experience only some isolated stress symptoms or other responses to vicarious trauma that do not neatly fit in a classic traumatic stress model. Little consideration, however, has been given to the nature of any such personal, partner, or relationship variables that may constitute a protective buffer for secondary survivors beyond perceived social support (Burgoff, 1993) and personal abuse history (Nelson and Wampler, 2000; 2002).

Further empirical study is also needed to understand the experiences of secondary survivors of childhood sexual abuse who are in relationships of various sexual, affectional, and permanency statuses. There was some initial support within the present study for previous observations concerning the impact of the "double secret" of lesbianism and childhood sexual abuse as it manifests itself in adult relationships (Hall, 1999). For example, based on extensive clinical experience, Smolover (1996) noted that, although many of the sequelae of childhood sexual abuse are quite similar regardless of the gender composition of the couple, lesbian couples are distinct in having two members who were socialized as women. As a result, Smolover suggested that these couples' issues may be complicated by their expected roles as caretakers, difficulties in establishing boundaries versus merging, or problems expressing anger, all of which were evidenced in this study for Pam and Angie, as well as by internalized homophobia.

By virtue of its small sample size, it should be emphasized that this study is preliminary and remains subject to the limitations of qualitative research in general. However, it also accrues the benefits of qualitative methodology, as reflected in the wealth of contextual data obtained and in the meaningfulness of the interview process as expressed by participants. As such, this study is not designed to be a representative portrayal of the sequelae of childhood sexual abuse generalizable to all secondary survivors or, for that matter, to the "typical" secondary survivor. Rather, the aim was to elucidate as many potential sequelae to childhood sexual abuse as possible for male partners as secondary survivors. These themes can then serve as the building blocks for theorizing about what the nature and extent of these sequelae may be under a variety of conditions, and what meaning this may have for individual secondary and primary survivors, for their relationships, and for the mental health professionals who work with them (Wiersma, 2003).

Finally, it should also be noted that participants in the present sample consisted largely of unmarried college students with a relatively short relationship duration. The interview process encouraged these couples to offer their perceptions and attributions regarding the sequelae of childhood sexual abuse for the secondary survivors, rather than implicating the abuse as a direct causal determinant of their actual present functioning. In addition, although the majority of participating primary survivors had recently sought treatment related to their abuse, none of their partners had sought such treatment related to their status as secondary survivors. As a result of these collective factors, both primary and secondary survivors in the present study were much more articulate regarding the longstanding sequelae of the abuse for primary survivors, and both primary and secondary survivors had difficulty characterizing the sequelae for secondary survivors. In discussing the secondary sequelae, participants frequently qualified their responses and relied more heavily on interviewer prompts, paraphrases, reflections, and clarifications, and all participants noted the novelty of discussing these issues. This response style in and of itself reflects the great need for further study of the sequelae of childhood sexual abuse for partners in a broader range of couples. These individuals should not remain forgotten victims, but are worthy of the careful study and informed assistance that will facilitate their growth into secondary survivors.

REFERENCES

American Psychiatric Association (1987). *Diagnostic and statistical manual of mental disorders* (3rd ed., revised). Washington, D. C.: Author.

American Psychiatric Association (1994). *Diagnostic and statistical manual of mental disorders* (4th ed.). Washington, D. C.: Author.

Bacon, B., and Lein, L. (1996). Living with a female sexual abuse survivor: Male partners' perspectives. *Journal of Child Sexual Abuse*, 5, 1-16.

Barcus, R. (1997). *Partners of survivors of abuse*: A men's therapy group. *Psychotherapy*, 34, 316-323.

Barnett, A. J. (1993). *Adult vicarious victims of child sexual abuse. Sexual and Marital Therapy*, 8, 75-80.

Bass, E., and Davis, L. (1988). *The courage to heal*: *A guide for women survivors of child sexual abuse*. New York: Harper and Row.

Bateman, A. W., and Mendelson, E. F. (1989). Sexual offences: Help for the forgotten victims. *Sexual and Marital Therapy*, 4, 5-7.

Beaton, R. D., and Murphy, S. a. (1995). *Working with people in crisis: Research implications*. In C. R. Figley (Ed.), Compassion fatigue: Coping with secondary traumatic stress disorder (pp. 51-81). New York: Brunner/Mazel.

Beitchman, J. H., Zucker, K. H., Hood, J. E., DaCosta, G. A., Akman, D., and Cassavia, E. (1992). *A review of the long-term effects of child sexual abuse. Child Abuse and Neglect*, 16, 101- 118.

Blume, S. (1990). *Secret survivors: Uncovering incest and its aftereffects in women*. New York: John Wiley and Sons.

Brittain, D. E., and Merriam, K. (1988). Groups for significant others of survivors of child sexual abuse. *Journal of Interpersonal Violence*, 3, 90-101.

Browne, A., and Finkelhor, D. (1986). Impact of child sexual abuse: A review of the research. *Psychological Bulletin*, 99, 66-77.

Burge, S. K., and Figley, C. R. (1987). The Social Support Scale: Development and initial estimates of reliability and validity. *Victimology*, 12, 14-22.

Burghoff, D. T. (1994). The relationship between well-being and social support among male partners of survivors of childhood sexual abuse. *Dissertation Abstract International*, 55(1-B), 6708.

Cahill, C., Llewelyn, S. P., and Pearson, C. (1991). Long-term effects of sexual abuse which occurred in childhood: A review. *British Journal of Clinical Psychology*, 30, 117-130.

Chauncey, S. (1994). Emotional concerns and treatment of male partners of female sexual abuse survivors. Social Work, 39, 669-676.

Chessick, R. D. (1978). *The sad soul of the psychiatrist.* Bulletin of the Menninger Clinic, 42, 1-9.

Cohen, L. J. (1988). Providing treatment and support for partners of sexual assault survivors. *Psychotherapy*, 25, 94-98.

Conte, J. R. (1985). The effects of sexual abuse on children: A critique and suggestions for future research. *Victimology*, 10, 110-130.

Davis, L. (1991). *Allies in healing: When the person you love was sexually abused as a child.* New York: Harper Collins.

Davis, R. C., and Friedman, L. N. (1985). *The emotional aftermath of crime and violence.* In C. R. Figley (Ed.), *Trauma and its wake: The study and treatment of post-traumatic stress disorder.* New York: Brunner/Mazel.

De Beixedon, S. Y. (1995). *Lovers and survivors: A partner's guide to living with and loving a sexual abuse survivor.* San Francisco: Robert D. Reed.

Drabek, T. E., Kay, W. H., Erickson, P. E., and Crowe, J. L. (1975). The impact of disaster on kin relationships. *Journal of Marriage and the Family*, 37, 481-497.

Emm, D. E., and McKenry, P. C. (1988). Coping with victimization: The impact of rape on female survivors, male significant others, and parents. *Contemporary Family Therapy*, 10, 272-279.

Engle, B. (1991). *Partners in recovery: How mates, lovers, and other prosurvivors can learn to support and cope with adult survivors of childhood sexual abuse.* Lowell House.

Ferguson, R. (1991). *Concerns and beliefs of male partners of female survivors of childhood sexual abuse: A qualitative study.* Unpublished manuscript, University of Kentucky, Lexington.

Ferguson, R. (1993). Male partners of female survivors of childhood sexual abuse: An inquiry into the concept of secondary victimization. (Doctoral Dissertation, University of Kentucky, Lexington, 1993). *Dissertation Abstracts International*, 54(9-B), 4915.

Figley, C. (1983). Catastrophes: An overview of family reactions. In C. R. Figley and H. L. McCubbin (Eds.), *Stress and the family* (Vol.2): *Coping with catastrophes*. New York: Brunner/Mazel.

Figley, C. (1986). *Trauma and its wake* (Vol. 2): Post traumatic stress disorder theory, research, and treatment. New York: Brunner/Mazel.

Figley, C. (1988a). A 5-phase treatment of family traumatic stress. *Journal of Traumatic Stress*, 1, 79-91.

Figley, C. (1988b). *Victimization, trauma, and traumatic stress*. Counseling Psychologist, 16, 635-641.

Figley, C. (1995). Compassion fatigues secondary traumatic stress disorder: An overview. In C. R. Figley (Ed.), *Compassion fatigue: Coping with secondary traumatic stress disorder* (pp. 1-20). New York: Brunner/Mazel.

Finkelhor, D. (1987). The trauma of child sexual abuse. *Journal of Interpersonal Violence*, 2, 348-365.

Firth, M. T. (1997). Male partners of female victims of child sexual abuse: Treatment issues and approaches. *Sexual and Marital Therapy*, 12, 159-171.

Ghahramanlou, M., and Brodbeck, C. (2000). Predictors of secondary trauma in sexual assault trauma counselors. *International Journal of Emergency Mental Health Special Issue*, 2, 229- 240.

Gil, E. (1993). *Outgrowing the pain together: A book for spouses and partners of adults abused as children*. New York: Dell.

Graber, K. (1991). *Ghosts in the bedroom: A guide for the partners of incest survivors*. Deerfield Beach, FL: Health Communications, Inc.

Green, A. H. (1993). Child sexual abuse: Immediate and long-term effects and intervention. *Journal of the American Academy of Child and Adolescent Psychiatry*, 32, 890-902.

Hall, J. (1999). An exploration of the sexual and relationship experiences of lesbian survivors of childhood sexual abuse. *Sexual and Marital Therapy*, 14, 61-70.

Hansen, P. A. (1991). *Survivors and partners: Healing the relationships of sexual abuse survivors*. Longmont, CO: Heron Hill Publishing.

Hartsough, D. (1985). *Stressors and supports for emergency workers:* The emergency organization role. In *National Institute of Mental Health* (Ed.), Role stressors and supports for emergency workers (pp. 48-58). Washington, D. C.: *National Institute of Mental Health*.

Harvey, J. H., Orbuch, T. L., Weber, A., Merbach, N., and Alt, R. (1992). House of pain and hope: Accounts of loss. *Death Studies*, 16, 88-124.

Hill, R. (1949). *Families under stress*. New York: Harper and Row.

Hill, C. E., Thompson, B. J., and Williams, E. N. (1997). A guide to conducting consensual qualitative research. *Counseling Psychologist,* 25, 517-572.

Jehu, D., Klassen, C., and Gazan, M. (1985). Common therapeutic targets among women who were sexually abused in childhood. *Journal of social Work and Human Sexuality,* 3, 25-45.

Kerewsky, D., and Miller, D. (1996). *Lesbian couples and childhood trauma: Guidelines for therapists.* In J. Laird and R. J. Green (Eds.), *Lesbians and gays in couples and families: A handbook for therapists.* San Francisco: Jossey-Bass.

Kilpatrick, A. C. (1987). Childhood sexual experiences: Problems and issues in studying long- range effects. *The Journal of Sex Research,* 23, 173-196.

Kisher, G. R., and Figley, C. R. (1987). *The relationship between psychiatric symptoms of crime victims and their supporters.* Unpublished manuscript.

Kroes, W. (1976). *Society's victim: The policeman.* Springfield, IL: Charles C. Thomas.

Kuhn, T. (1970). *The structure of scientific revolutions.* (2nd ed.). Chicago: University of Chicago Press.

Landry, D. B., and Bear, E. (1991). *Family fallout: A handbook for families of adult sexual abuse survivors.* Brandon, VT: Safer Society Press.

Lev-Wiesel, R., and Amir, M. (2001). Secondary traumatic stress, psychological distress, sharing of traumatic reminisces, and marital quality among spouses of Holocaust child survivors. *Journal of Marital and Family Therapy*, 27, 433-444.

Lincoln, Y., and Guba, E. (1985). Naturalistic inquiry. Beverly Hills, CA: Sage.

Lipp, M. R. (1980). *The bitter pill: Doctors, patients, and failed expectations.* New York: Harper and Row.

Luepker, E. T., and O'Brien, M. O. (1989). *Support groups for spouses.* In G. R. Schoener, J. H. Milgrom, J. C. Gonsiorek, E. T. Luepker, and R. M. Conroe (Eds.), *Psychotherapists' sexual involvement with clients: Intervention and prevention* (pp. 241-244). Minneapolis: Walk-In Counseling Center.

Maltas, C., and Shay, J. (1995). Trauma contagion in partners of survivors of childhood sexual abuse. *American Journal of Orthopsychiatry*, 65, 529-539.

Maltz, W. (1988). Identifying and treating the sexual repercussions of incest: A couples therapy approach. *Journal of Sex and Marital Therapy,* 14, 142-170.

Maltz, W., and Holman, B. (1990). *Incest and sexuality: A guide to understanding and healing.* Lexington, MA: Lexington Books.

Marshall, C., and Rossman, G. B. (1995). *Designing qualitative research.* Thousand Oaks: Sage.

McCann, L., and Pearlman, L. (1990). Vicarious traumatization: A framework for understanding the psychological effects of working with victims. *Journal of Traumatic Stress, 3*, 131-149.

Miller, R. M., and Sutherland, K. J. (1999). Partners in healing: Systemic therapy with survivors of sexual abuse and their partners. *Journal of Family Studies, 5*, 97-111.

Mitchell, J. T. (1985). *Healing the helper. In National Institute of Mental Health (Ed.), Role stressors and supports for emergency workers* (pp. 105-118). Washington, D.C.: National Institute of Mental Health.

Myers, D. G. (1992). The pursuit of happiness. *Journal of Personality and Social Psychology, 59*, 762-769.

Nelson, B. S., and Wampler, K. S. (2002). Further understanding the systemic effects of childhood sexual abuse: A comparison of two groups of clinical couples. *Journal of Child Sexual Abuse, 11*, 85-106.

Neumann, D. A., Houskamp, B. M., Pollock, V. E., and Briere, J. (1996). *The long-term sequelae of childhood sexual abuse in women: A meta-analytic review.* Child Maltreatment, 1, 6-16.

Nelson, B. S., and Wampler, K. S. (2000). Systemic effects of trauma in clinic couples: An exploratory study of secondary trauma resulting from childhood abuse. *Journal of Marital and Family Therapy, 26*, 171-184.

Pearlman, L. A., and Saakvitne, K. W. (1995). *Trauma and the therapist: Countertransference and vicarious traumatization in psychotherapy with incest survivors.* New York: W. W. Norton and Company.

Pilisuk, M., and Parks, S. H. (1986). *The healing web: Social networks and human survival.* Hanover, NH: University Press of New England.

Reid, K., Mathews, G. and Liss, P. S. (1995). M*y partner is hurting: Group work with male partners of adult survivors of sexual abuse.* Social Work with Groups, 18, 81-87.

Reid, K. S., Wampler, R. S., and Taylor, D. K. (1996). The "alienated" partner: Responses to traditional therapies for adult sex abuse survivors. *Journal of Marital and Family Therapy, 22*, 443-453.

Remer, R. (1990). *Secondary victim/secondary survivor.* Unpublished manuscript, University of Kentucky, Lexington.

Remer, R., and Elliott, J. E. (1988a). Management of secondary victims of sexual assault. *International Journal of Family Psychiatry, 9*, 389-401.

Remer, R., and Elliott, J. E. (1988b). Characteristics of secondary victims of sexual assault. *International Journal of Family Psychiatry, 9*, 373-387.

Remer, R., and Ferguson, R. A. (1993). *Treating partners of primary trauma victims: Producing secondary survivors of PTSD*. In C. Figley (Ed.), Trauma and its wake (Vol. 3). New York: Brunner/Mazel.

Rodkin, L., Hunt, E., and Cowan, S. (1982). A men's support group for significant others of rape victims. *Journal of Marital and Family Therapy*, 8, 91-97.

Rose, K. D., and Rosow, I. (1973). *Physicians who kill themselves. Archives of General*

Psychiatry, 29, 800-805.

Russell, D. E. H. (1986). *The secret trauma: Incest in the lives of girls and women*. New York: Basic Books.

Sexton, L. (1999). Vicarious traumatisation of counsellors and effects on their workplaces. *British Journal of Guidance and Counselling*, 27, 393-403.

Sheldrick, C. (1991). Adult sequelae of child sexual abuse. *British Journal of Psychiatry*, 158, 55-62.

Silverman, D. C. (1978). Sharing the crisis of rape: Counseling the mates and families of victims. *American Journal of Orthopsychiatry*, 48, 166-173.

Silverman, D. C. (1992). *Male co-survivors: The shared trauma of rape*. In G. C. Mezey and M. B. King (Eds.), *Male victims of sexual assault* (pp. 87-103). Oxford: Oxford University Press.

Smolover, M. (1996). What about my needs? Working with lesbian partners of childhood sexual abuse survivors. In Christopher J. Alexander (Ed.), *Gay and lesbian mental health: A sourcebook for practitioners*. Binghamton, NY: Haworth Press.

Snyder, C. R., and Lopez, S. J. (2002). *Handbook of positive psychology*. Oxford: Oxford University Press.

Spear, J. (1991). *How can I help her? A handbook for partners of women sexually abused as children*. City Center, MN: Hazelden Foundation.

Stark, K. (1993). *Helping the adult survivor of child sexual abuse: For friends, family, and lovers*. Racine, WI: Mother Courage Press.

Strauss, A., and Corbin, J. (1990). *Basics of qualitative research: Grounded theory procedures and techniques*. Newbury Park: Sage.

Summey, J. R. (2001). The prevention, treatment, and mitigation of secondary traumatic stress in emergency personnel dealing with disasters. *Annals of the American Psychotherapy Association*, 4, 18-21.

Tedeschi, R. G., Park, C. L., and Calhoun, L. G. (1998). *Posttraumatic growth: Positive changes in the aftermath of crisis. Mahwah*, NJ: Lawrence Erlbaum.

Wiersma, N. S. (1999). Partner agreement regarding the adult sequelae of childhood sexual abuse for female survivors and their relationship partners.(Doctoral dissertation, Southern Illinois University at Carbondale, 1999). *Dissertation Abstracts International*, 60(3-B), 1353.

Wiersma, N. S. (2003). Partner awareness regarding the adult sequelae of childhood sexual abuse for primary and secondary survivors. *Journal of Marital and Family Therapy,* 29, 151-164.

INDEX

A

academics, 70
accounting, 6, 79
adjustment, 2, 6, 18, 29, 31, 82
adulthood, 1, 5, 6, 9, 81, 83
adults, 83, 89
advertisements, 16
affect, 3, 8, 28, 29, 30, 32, 33, 39, 82
age, 6, 9, 11, 14, 16
alcohol, 54, 56, 81
alienation, 13
ambiguity, 11, 34
American Psychiatric Association, 7, 87
amnesia, 8
anger, 5, 9, 11, 12, 13, 14, 15, 17, 26, 28, 43, 46, 51, 84
anxiety, 5, 11, 17, 54, 81
argument, 73
arousal, 1, 8
assault, 16, 88, 89, 91, 92
assessment, 16, 21, 39, 82
association, 1
attention, 1, 3, 7, 11, 67, 68, 69, 70, 71, 75, 81
attitudes, 10, 15, 60
auditing, 14
autonomy, 11
avoidance, 5, 8, 13, 15, 80
awareness, 15, 21, 22, 39, 62, 63, 75, 77, 80, 93

B

bad day, 64
barriers, 22
behavior, 3, 5, 10, 12, 51
blame, 32, 36, 59, 61, 66
brain, 40
building blocks, 84

C

catastrophes, 89
causal relationship, 4, 55
child abuse, 5
childhood sexual abuse, 1, 2, 3, 4, 5, 6, 8, 9, 10, 11, 13, 14, 15, 16, 17, 18, 19, 21, 22, 25, 26, 29, 34, 38, 39, 42, 43, 44, 48, 52, 54, 55, 57, 63, 68, 71, 79, 81, 82, 83, 84, 88, 89, 90, 91, 92, 93
children, 2, 7, 12, 15, 72, 83, 88, 89, 92
Christianity, 15
classes, 70
clients, 90
clinical syndrome, 82
coding, 22
cognition, 3
cohesion, 18
college students, 84
commitment, 10, 79
communication, 9, 13, 14, 17

E

D

F

T

V

W

Y